MW00915937

Critical Accountability– Updated for Remote Work!

Identify, Address, and Resolve Crucial Workplace Behavior and Productivity Issues by Learning to Effectively Culture Accountability and Improve Emotional Intelligence in Your Team

Gary Peterson

© Copyright 2021 - All rights reserved.

The content contained within this book may not be reproduced, duplicated, or transmitted without direct written permission from the author or the publisher.

Under no circumstances will any blame or legal responsibility be held against the publisher, or author, for any damages, reparation, or monetary loss due to the information contained within this book, either directly or indirectly.

Legal Notice:

This book is copyright protected. It is only for personal use. You cannot amend, distribute, sell, use, quote, or paraphrase any part, or the content within this book, without the consent of the author or publisher.

Disclaimer Notice:

Please note the information contained within this document is for educational and entertainment purposes only. All effort has been executed to present accurate, up-to-date, reliable, complete information. No warranties of any kind are declared or implied. Readers acknowledge that the author is not engaged in the rendering of legal, financial, medical, or professional advice. The content within this book has been derived from various sources. Please consult a licensed professional before attempting any techniques outlined in this book.

By reading this document, the reader agrees that under no circumstances is the author responsible for any losses, direct or indirect, that are incurred as a result of the use of the information contained within this document, including, but not limited to, errors, omissions, or inaccuracies.

Table of Contents

Introduction

"Accountability is the glue that ties commitment to the result."

-   *Bob Proctor*

Accountability is a crucial part of personal and professional integrity, ethics, and success. The problem is that too few people hold themselves or others accountable in a world that seems to constantly be coming up with more and more excuses. You see your friends do it, your coworkers do it, celebs do it, even politicians and world leaders do it. You might even do it too.

We have built a culture of complacency that views responsibility as an unpleasant chore instead of a vital part of life. This lack of accountability can seriously hurt your team and your organization as a whole. It's something many organizational leaders want to stamp out but how do you go about doing that? Hold onto your seat because I'm going to show you how.

In this book, I've compiled all the information you need to build a culture of accountability in your team. I'm even going to tell you how to whip yourself into accountable shape. After all, accountability starts with you. Before you can hold anybody else accountable, you need to be accountable for your own decisions.

In this book, I'm going to reveal:

- The true definition of accountability.

- How accountability, responsibility, trust, and assertiveness all tie in together.

- How to assess your own accountability.

- How to improve personal accountability and build it in your staff.

- Why and how emotional intelligence is a vital part of accountability.

- How to confront a lack of accountability in someone else.

- How to create a culture of accountability in your team, even if it's virtual.

- And much, much more.

You can turn a team with accountability issues into one that is astoundingly functional with the right tools. If you've had enough of the accountability issues in your organization, it's time for a change. Your productivity and success will skyrocket when everybody accepts responsibility for their own actions and the results they produce. So, without further ado, let's find out how to turn things around and build an accountable team and organization.

Chapter 1:

Defining and

Understanding

Accountability

You may have heard phrases like "Someone needs to be held accountable for..." or, in a business sense, "The company is not being held accountable for..." Most of us have a general, possibly even vague, understanding of what accountability means. To master holding yourself and others accountable, the concept needs to be clearly defined. A clear definition leaves no wiggle room for ineffective accountability practices as a result of misunderstandings.

Accountability Defined

So, let's get down to business by starting with a definition of accountability:

"An obligation or willingness to accept responsibility or to account for one's actions." (Merriam-Webster, n.d.)

Whatever you do in any sphere of your life, accountability requires you to take responsibility for what you do or don't do. Inaction is just as much a part of accountability as action. For example, if you say you are going to do something but don't do it, you are still responsible for not taking action. Truly taking accountability for yourself means owning up to your actions without making excuses, no 'but' involved.

When I say no excuses, what I mean is trying to dig yourself out of a hole you've gotten yourself into by playing the blame game; finding a reason not to take responsibility. The classic schoolyard excuse "My dog ate my homework" is a perfect example. What I don't mean is providing a legitimate reason for the action, "I did not complete my homework because I was involved in an accident while riding my bike home and spent the afternoon at the hospital." See how you own up to not having done what was expected of you by providing a legitimate reason? Taking accountability should also be followed up with a solution, such as "Given extra time, I will put in the effort to complete my homework." Coming up with a solution shows you are still taking responsibility.

Accountability is a three-part concept. To be held accountable by others, or even yourself, there must be:

- An obligation: Without an obligation, you don't have to take responsibility or be held accountable for your actions.

- An action: Accountability requires you to either do or not do something expected of you, but it extends further than just the results of that action. It involves how those results are achieved.

- Someone to hold you accountable: For accountability to be effective, there must be someone who is holding you accountable. It may be someone else or it could even be yourself.

Let's review the action part of accountability for a moment. I said it's not just a case of getting something done, it's also about how it gets done. You may be wondering, "Who cares how it gets done as long as it gets done, right?" Not quite. Taking another look at the classic homework example I used above; how you get your homework done is just as important as getting it done. Simply scribbling down an essay or answers to questions to get it out of the way as quickly as possible gets it done, sure. However, the quality of your homework is going to be sub-par. The obligation wasn't just to do it, it was to do it to the best of your ability. Now that we have this cleared up, it's time to move on to another important aspect of understanding what accountability really means.

Accountability vs. Responsibility

The definition of accountability includes the word 'responsibility' which is probably why the two are often used interchangeably and confused with each other. Responsibility and accountability are two different things. They work hand-in-hand, though. Here's where it gets tricky. You can be both accountable and responsible for an action or you could be accountable for what gets done and how it's done but not responsible for doing it. If that sounds confusing, don't worry, I'm going to clear it all up.

Accountability and responsibility part ways when it comes to delegation. More often than not, this is encountered in a business and management scenario. A manager is accountable for ensuring the staff working under them get tasks done and how they do it but they are not responsible for the actual doing. The staff member performing the task is responsible for the action that needs to be taken to produce the results. The manager holds the employee accountable for their actions contributing to the results and the manager is held accountable for delivering those results and how the employee achieves them.

This is the part where I "bake your noodle." The manager is not responsible for the actions employees take to deliver the expected results, but they are responsible for their own actions in the chain of events leading up to producing those results. Wait, what? I just said they are accountable for the results being achieved but not the actions taken by contributing staff members so how are they responsible for any actions? The manager is responsible for the actions they take to hold employees accountable by:

- Communicating obligations and consequences clearly.

- Monitoring tasks, methods, and progress.

- Consistently implementing consequences for inaction or poor performance.

Another difference between responsibility and accountability is how responsible you feel for your actions. In this way, your own sense of responsibility will influence how accountable you feel you are. After all, if you don't feel you are responsible for doing something and doing it well, you won't feel strongly accountable for the action or the results.

Once again, I'm going to revisit that homework excuse. You might be wondering why I keep returning to the same example, isn't it getting tired by now? I like to be consistent with our examples, offering you better clarity about what I'm trying to relate to you as opposed to using a bunch of different examples which could become confusing in the long run.

Let's break down this demonstration of the difference and interconnection between responsibility and accountability to detangle and clarify each point.

- Your teacher is held accountable by the school and your parents to provide you with a quality education and ensure you get good grades.

- Despite the teacher being held accountable for the ultimate results, you, as the student, are responsible for your actions that lead to the results.

- Your teacher, while not responsible for your actions, contributes to the result which includes providing quality education through good teaching practices and creating a positive learning environment. They are also responsible for clearly communicating what they expect of you and then consistently applying consequences if you don't meet those expectations to a reasonable and satisfactory standard.

- Responsibility and accountability come back together when the teacher holds you accountable for your actions and the results you achieve.

As you can see, responsibility and accountability can be both inextricably intertwined and separate. They coexist on multiple levels and to varying degrees, making accountability a complex concept to wrap your head around and implement from both a personal and authoritative perspective. Now that you've gained better insight into what accountability is, let's dive into the role of accountability within organizations.

The Role of Accountability in Organizational Success

Accountability is pivotal to the success of any organization. Without it, everything begins to unravel. What role does accountability play in management and leadership and how does it affect organizational success?

Improving Performance

For any business to be successful, it has to perform well. Performance is improved when a culture of accountability is created within the organization. This contributes to the overall culture of the company, creating a sense of belonging by valuing the individual as well as the team which increases employee participation and support of communal goals. It also helps build and establish trust while improving tolerance and acceptance.

Without accountability, performance nosedives. Individual and team senses of responsibility evaporates;

everybody blames everybody else for shortcomings. When individuals and teams aren't held accountable for their decisions and actions, it becomes a situation of "I'm not responsible for the company's underperformance" by way of "It's not my fault, it's someone else's." Another mentality that develops is "It doesn't matter if I don't do a good job because there will be no consequences anyway." These ways of thinking breed underachievement which affects productivity and revenue.

Maintaining Structure and Order

Proper accountability in an organization is crucial to maintaining structure and order in the company. However, laying blame everywhere else undermines workplace trust and relationships. Teams become disjointed when members don't trust each other and are always pointing fingers at others or watching their back in case a finger is pointed at them. Even the organization's management hierarchy is jeopardized when subordinates blame management for non-productivity. The structure of the company is destabilized which only drags performance and success down further.

Improving Compliance

This is one you may not think about when considering the role of accountability in organizations. Compliance covers a wide range of overall company responsibilities, such as:

- Abiding by health and safety regulations.

- Keeping to fair labor practices.

- Preventing oversights.

- Following the letter of the law.

When individuals and teams are held accountable for decisions and actions, the organization is more likely to adhere to compliance across the field. This compliance improves organizational credibility, performance, and success.

Improving Trust and Respect of Management

This is where personal accountability on behalf of management comes into play alongside holding others accountable. When management, or a member of management, loses the trust and respect of the staff working under them, disaster soon follows. This particular role of accountability in organizational success encompasses all the other roles I've just mentioned. The power of management is key to the performance, structure, and culture of a company.

Management is only granted this power when they hold themselves accountable for their own decisions and actions and constantly hold staff accountable. This grows trust between management and staff that consequences will consistently be doled out for lack of performance and management will also admit to making mistakes and work toward improving their own performance. Good management starts with accountability.

The Big PA: Personal Accountability

In the previous section, I touched on the importance of personal accountability in management and leadership. Personal accountability has a vital hand to play in both your personal and professional life, even if you aren't in a leadership position. When it comes to accountability in every aspect of life, the buck starts and ends with you. This isn't to say that taking accountability for your decisions and actions will guarantee your relationships and the company you work for will be successful. Those situations involve more than one person and depend on a variety of factors, but taking personal accountability goes a long way to make sure you do everything you can to make a success of it. Furthermore, personal accountability is a huge contributing factor to achieving your personal goals in life.

Ask yourself one poignant question, "How can I hold others accountable if I don't hold myself accountable?"

Accountability presents itself in eight levels, also called the "accountability ladder." This ladder represents varying degrees of personal accountability. When making your way up this ladder, keep in mind that accountability isn't just about getting things done or not; it's how willing you are to take responsibility for your actions to fulfill an obligation. The accountability ladder starts with the highest level of accountability as the top rung and the least accountability at the bottom.

8. "I'm going to do whatever it takes to get this done successfully."

7. "I'm going to find a solution to this challenge."

6. "I accept what needs to be done or changed, and I acknowledge and accept the role I have to play in it."

5. "I accept what needs to be done or the changes that need to be made to solve a problem."

4. "I'm just going to wait and see what happens. Maybe it'll just go away by itself without me having to do anything about it."

3. "My lack of accountability is justifiable. I can rationalize my way out of this."

2. "It's not my fault. That person/equipment/circumstance is to blame."

1. "I'm completely unaware of what is expected of me."

Levels one to four of the accountability ladder represent people who have a poor sense, or complete lack, of accountability. Levels five through eight represent people with moderate to high accountability.

People with a low level of accountability tend to have a victim mentality. You know someone–perhaps even yourself– who has this way of thinking. Excuses, such as the following, often crop up in the face of being held accountable:

- "It's not my fault."

- "I didn't know it needed to get done." or "I didn't know it needed to be done by.../in that way."

- "I wasn't told what to do/how to do it."

- "It's not my responsibility/job/department."

- "I've always done it this way."

- "But I forgot to..."

- "Nobody reminded me to..."

- "I don't know."

- "I was too busy."

Poor accountability is often defended by the use of the word "but." Let's explore the damaging effect of excuses and why you should ditch them, effective immediately.

Ditch the Excuse Habit

How often do you make excuses for your actions or inaction? Do you realize you are making them? Excuses are the stories we use to rationalize and validate our actions or failures. The process of making an excuse involves:

1. Finding a reason for your action, even if it's not a very good reason at all.

2. Convincing yourself the reason is viable, rational, and reasonable.

3. Selling your excuse to the person holding you accountable, even if that's yourself.

Selling excuses to others is only half of the problem. The other half is accepting excuses. It can sometimes seem easier to allow others' actions or failures to slide by accepting their excuses and letting them off the hook. Just as making excuses yourself doesn't build your personal accountability, allowing others to get off scot-free by accepting excuses doesn't encourage them to take accountability either. Excuses are a way of denying personal accountability, whether it's your own or someone else's, and personal accountability on an individual level is the root of all organizational accountability problems.

Exercise: To begin ditching the habit of making excuses, you first need to realize you're making them and how often it happens. You also have to realize how often you are accepting them. Spend a week paying close attention to your interactions with others. Make notes of how often you make and accept excuses. During the week, you will undoubtedly try to move away from making and/or accepting excuses because this exercise is drawing your attention to them. Even if you choose not to make an excuse, if you felt the impulse to do it, make a note of it to give you a true reflection of how often you would normally make or accept excuses.

Understanding Excuses

It's easier to give up a bad habit when you understand why it exists in the first place. There are several reasons people make excuses in different situations. Understanding why you're making an excuse can be the key to unlocking the courage to resist falling into the trap.

Shirking Responsibility

Responsibility is hard. There are no two ways about it. Taking responsibility for yourself, your actions, and your decisions is a tough business. It requires you to challenge yourself and own up to mistakes and failures. Shirking that responsibility by making excuses may seem like an easy way out but it may be more costly than you think. What is the consequence of not taking responsibility? You develop self-limiting beliefs and deny yourself opportunities to learn and grow.

Fear

Fear is a powerful motivation for making excuses. Fear motivates you to make excuses for your actions or for declining responsibility. You may fear failure or embarrassment if you take on responsibility. You might be fearful of what others will think of you if you allow yourself to be held accountable for your actions, mistakes, or failures. When fear is the motivation behind making excuses, it may be rooted in self-doubt, self-esteem, and emotional intelligence, but we'll tackle these topics in the next chapter.

Overcommitting

You're bound to overburden yourself by taking on more than you can manage if you can't say "no." Being unable to decline requests and be assertive in your communication with friends, family, and in the workplace could also be due to fear. You may fear what others will think if you say no to them. You may be trying to impress your boss at work. Perhaps you don't want to disappoint someone or hurt their feelings. Maybe you just don't want to appear rude.

Committing to challenging demands in your professional or personal life provides you with a chance to grow and learn. However, overcommitting stretches you beyond your limits and ultimately, your self-worth and how others view you will take a knock when you can't stick to those commitments. We'll explore assertiveness in the next chapter to help you avoid overcommitting.

A Conflict of Values

Often a conflict will come into play when you've committed to something that doesn't align with your personal values. Your values offer motivation to get things done, but when you remove that motivation, you may find yourself making excuses for not doing something or not putting in the effort needed to succeed. In a case of conflicting values, assertive communication will help you avoid committing to or doing anything that doesn't align with, or even goes against your values, in the first place.

A Lack of Motivation

Your values offer some motivation but that's only one piece of the puzzle. Other sources of motivation include personal desires and goals. When you aren't motivated to do something, you're less likely to do it or to do it well, even if you decide to do it in the first place. Motivation is important both in your personal and professional life. If you aren't motivated to get ahead in your career, you're likely to make excuses and avoid accepting accountability for poor performance. If you aren't motivated to work on interpersonal relationships with friends and family, you're probably not going to stick to commitments and promises.

Protecting Your Sense of Self

Freud would call your sense of self your ego. The above reasons illustrate situations in which we make excuses, but the driving force behind making excuses is to protect our sense of self. Being held accountable for an action or failure may seem like an attack on our self-perception or how we view ourselves. Self-perception can be a delicate thing; our egos can easily be bruised.

Let's go back to that homework example again. Your teacher questions why your homework wasn't done to a satisfactory standard. You're suddenly put on the spot, you may feel embarrassed, you may feel you are being criticized, and you may even feel indignant. Your excuse may be that the assignment was too hard or unfair. You may make the excuse that you weren't feeling well. In these instances, you are shifting the focus from your actions to an external factor, which frames the results as being out of your control. You're trying to convince yourself, and your teacher, it's not you, it's something else. By doing this, you are avoiding dealing with uncomfortable emotions such as embarrassment, anxiety, fear, and shame. In the next chapter, we'll delve into emotional intelligence and why it's so important for dealing with difficult emotions and accepting accountability.

The Cost of Excuses

Making excuses may help protect your ego and deflect difficult emotions like embarrassment but they also come at a price. There are various ways in which excuses are costing you more than you may realize.

You're Robbed of Potential and Opportunity

Making excuses to avoid taking responsibility and avoid challenging yourself robs you of the chance to grow and reach your full potential. Accepting excuses from others and cleaning up their messes has a similar effect, forcing you to shift your focus, time, and energy to accepting unnecessary responsibility.

You're Limiting Yourself

Making excuses not to do something or for mistakes and failures creates self-limiting beliefs and reinforces self-doubt. You remain in your comfort zone and even restrict it. You are stopping yourself from living a fulfilling life you are happy with. As much as excuses may help you avoid anxiety and uncomfortable situations, they are also keeping you stuck in situations that are making you unhappy or anxious.

Your Credibility Suffers

When you're always using excuses to rationalize your actions, mistakes, or failures, you're slowly chipping away at your credibility. Eventually, all those people you've been making excuses to stop believing them and start expecting more of the same in the future. Your reliability goes down the drain; the only thing people can rely on is that you'll have an excuse. This loss of credibility happens in both your personal and professional life, putting strain on your interpersonal relationships with everybody you interact with.

You Encourage Others

The moment you make it okay to make excuses, you are setting the stage for others to follow by example. People are social creatures. One of the aspects of living as social beings is the knock-on effect. What you do influences others and what others do influences you. This happens in personal relationships and the workplace, especially if you are in a management position. When management comes up with excuses to evade or sidestep accountability, other employees get the message that it's okay to make excuses. When parents make excuses, children learn the same bad habit.

Accountability and Trust

Accountability and trust go hand-in-hand. There cannot be trust without accountability and accountability requires trust; whether it's in a personal relationship or an organizational team.

A highly accountable person builds trust by:

- Doing what they say they will do when it needs to be done.

- Owning up to making mistakes and failing without making excuses or laying blame at the feet of others.

- Engaging in problem-solving to find solutions to challenges or overcome mistakes.

- Taking action to make amends and ensure obstacles are navigated for success.

Accountability is also closely linked to reliability which is linked to trust. Being highly accountable to yourself and others means you can be relied on, people can trust you and take your word without wondering whether you're going to do it or if you'll do a good job of it. That's the first and most obvious reason accountability builds and strengthens trust.

When you dig deeper, you discover spin-off reasons low levels of accountability can destroy trust, especially in the workplace. Being unreliable often means missed deadlines and poor performance. This breeds contempt among team members. If even one member of a team has poor accountability, everyone suffers and animosity threatens to overthrow team harmony. Your team essentially becomes dysfunctional and you'll probably hear grumblings among members who are dissatisfied with always being dragged down by the poor accountability of an element of the team. Even more sinister are suspicion and retaliation. As we've learned, people who do not take accountability for their actions are quick to make excuses, even if it means blaming someone who isn't really at fault. It puts the entire team on edge, increasing tension as each person is constantly watching their back in case blame is slung at them out of the blue. When accusations and blame are hurled around a team, trust disintegrates and hostility may even set in, further weakening the cohesion and performance of the team.

Assessing Accountability

As I explained earlier, making excuses to avoid taking accountability is often linked to a desire to protect your sense of self from being undermined. So it stands to reason that your perception of your own level of accountability may not be quite as accurate as you think. However, before you can start working on being more accountable, you need to know where you currently stand on the accountability scale. The following questionnaire will help you figure out how accountable you really are versus how accountable you think you are.

Instructions:

Read the 20 statements below and provide a rating using the rating guide provided. Be brutally honest with yourself. Once you have rated each statement, tally up your scores to get an overall score which you can then use to determine how accountable you are based on the scoring guideline at the bottom of the questionnaire.

1. Never
2. Rarely
3. Sometimes
4. Usually
5. Always

Statements	1	2	3	4	5
I know when I need to get permission to do something and when I am responsible for deciding to do something.					
When I am not given clear direction, I clarify or find out what I need to do.					
When getting things done, I set up my own procedures and timeframes.					
I complete everything I set out to do.					
I do what I am supposed to do, even when I'm not being watched.					
I know how to source the information I need to do things.					
If I don't know something, I let others					

Statements	1	2	3	4	5
know.					
I am proactive about getting feedback from others.					
I get to know those around me so I can get help if I need it.					
I look for different ways to evaluate my knowledge and abilities.					
I do what I say I am going to do, no excuses.					
I can challenge and manage negative thoughts and emotions.					
I don't expect anything I haven't earned.					
I take ownership of the results of my actions and decisions.					
When I face challenges, I find solutions.					
I can give "progress reports" for both my personal and professional lives.					

Statements	1	2	3	4	5
I take pride in the fact that I produce a consistent and reliable level of quality.					
I know what motivates me and use methods to keep myself motivated.					
I have ways of keeping myself on track in both my personal and professional lives.					
I know how to move forward if I get derailed.					
Totals for each column:					
Total overall score:					

Scoring Guideline:

- Less than 50: You have a low accountability level.

- 50-70: You have a medium accountability level.

- 70-90: You are fairly accountable.

- More than 90: You are a highly accountable person.

In addition to the statement questionnaire above, here are a few more statements you can use to determine your own level of accountability. Unlike the assessment above, these statements will only point you in a general direction. You could also use these statements to evaluate how accountable your staff feels they are by asking them to rate how strongly the statements resonate with them on a scale of 1 to 10.

- I accept accountability for what I do and the results of my actions.

- I hold myself accountable for my own performance.

- I hold others accountable for their actions or performance.

- I shift accountability to colleagues or someone higher up.

- I face challenges willingly.

- I take responsibility for the results of facing challenges and obstacles.

- I'm not keen on taking on new responsibilities.

- I am reluctant to face challenges.

- I set actionable, attainable goals.

- I follow through on reaching my goals.

- I own my mistakes and failures.

- If I don't meet expectations, I find a reason to use as an excuse.

- I use problem-solving to resolve mistakes I've made.

- I'm not a leader, I would rather follow.

- I try to explain my poor performance to justify it.

Improving Personal Accountability

Improving personal accountability isn't going to happen overnight. Some aspects of developing personal accountability can only be addressed by working on your emotional intelligence, which I'll get into in the next chapter. However, there are a few habits you can start forming today that will help you on your way to becoming fully accountable.

Understand and Admit Your Limits

We all have limitations and that's not a bad thing. Your limits only put your personal accountability in jeopardy if you don't know what they are and if you don't admit you have them. Before accepting and committing to anything, consider these things:

- Do you have the resources, knowledge, and skills to do it?

- Do you have the time to do it without missing the deadline?

Communicate honestly and openly with whoever it is you're dealing with, whether that's your spouse, family, friends, work colleagues, or even your boss. Being open about what you already have on your plate helps the other person understand why you're not prepared to commit. You are also opening yourself up for feedback, putting your heads together to come up with solutions, and being seen as a person of integrity.

Manage Your Time

Everybody knows how crucial time management is in the workplace but they can overlook how important it is in your personal life as well. Learning good time management skills will help you avoid getting stuck between a rock and a hard place by running out of time. Managing your time well will also allow you to be aware of your limits and when you can or can't commit to doing something.

Know What You're Committing To

How can you hold yourself accountable, or be held accountable by someone else, if you don't know exactly what you are agreeing to do? Clear communication is a vital part of establishing your accountability for tasks or behaviors. You need to know exactly what is expected of you and if you aren't certain, ask for clarity.

Look After Yourself

Mental and physical health also play a role in your accountability. A healthy body and mind increase productivity, creativity, problem-solving, decision-making, focus, motivation, and other functions which are all vital for establishing your own accountability.

Ask for Feedback/Help/Advice

When you ask for feedback and keep yourself open to change, you are holding the door open for continuous learning. Not all feedback is criticism, and doing the same thing the same way you've always done it keeps you stuck in a rut. Asking for feedback or advice brings a fresh perspective into play which may help with your problem-solving skills. You could get guidance on how to improve your efficiency by doing something differently; improving your accountability. When you stop asking for advice, you stop learning and growing while the world keeps moving forward around you. Changing with the times can only help you bump up your accountability.

Identify Your Weaknesses

There are more things that could be standing in your way of improving your personal accountability than there are pages in this book. They could range from mental attitudes to a lack of skills to bad habits like procrastinating or getting distracted easily. Identifying your weaknesses is the first step to dealing with them. Once you know what they are, you can find ways to remove those obstacles from your path.

Evaluating Workplace Accountability

Assessing your personal accountability helps you get a better idea of where you stand on the accountability scale, but what about your workplace? When you hold a managerial position, personal accountability is key. You can't expect others to be accountable to you if you aren't accountable yourself. However, workplace accountability goes deeper than just working on holding yourself and others accountable within the organization. Workplace accountability is more than just action, it's also a feeling. When your staff don't feel the management or company as a whole is accountable, they will wonder why they should be accountable and their own accountability is more likely to slip.

Building a culture of accountability is, therefore, vitally important to organizational success and employee satisfaction. I'll reveal how to build that organization-wide accountability in a later chapter. For now, let's evaluate the level of accountability in your organization based on your own perception as part of management and employee perception. Getting staff feedback on how accountable they feel various teams or departments are will offer you an insight into where employees feel accountability can be beefed up. As they say, two heads are better than one. In the case of assessing organizational accountability, multiple heads give a clearer picture of what is really going on.

How do you go about assessing organization-wide accountability? Survey questionnaires are perfect for gathering staff feedback. They also serve more than one purpose. Not only are you receiving information from your employees, you're also providing staff members with the actions and results that the company expects of them.

Questionnaire One

There are seven vital statements to put to yourself and your staff about accountability to help measure the level on an individual basis and across the company. While these are statements, they can also be framed as questions.

I have a goal-oriented plan in place for my career and I'm working toward achieving those goals. This question tackles the topic of motivation to be accountable for your actions. Without motivation, accountability becomes a moot point. Why would you want to take responsibility and be answerable for actions and outcomes you aren't really interested in?

I know what I do helps the company reach its goals. Answering this question speaks to individual personal accountability by giving you an idea of whether staff members understand how what they do helps the company reach its goals. Without a proper understanding of their contribution to the business's success, employees may not feel they should take responsibility for their actions because they don't know if what they're doing actually matters all that much.

As a team/department, we hold ourselves and our colleagues accountable for their actions and the outcomes. Notice how this question uses "we." People naturally gravitate toward providing answers that will make them fit in with the expectations of the question. If they answer truthfully about their lack of accountability, they may fear being picked on or singled out as being a "bad apple." Putting the question in a "we" context generally returns a more honest answer about how employees perceive accountability across the board.

Management is held accountable for their actions and overall organizational success. It's not just about measuring how accountable they and their teammates are. How accountable they feel management is will affect their willingness to be accountable for their own actions.

If I need resources I don't already have, I ask for what I need to do to be able to reach personal

career and company-oriented goals. What does this question tell you about an employee? How is asking for additional resources important to accountability? Owning your actions is part of accountability. Asking for what you need indicates you're willing to own the job to make a success of it.

I regularly ask for feedback from my colleagues and superiors. Again, this question tells you about an individual's willingness to take responsibility for their work. Requesting feedback means they are taking the reins and proactively looking for ways to improve instead of staying stuck in the rut of "This is how I've always done it."

I look for chances to gain and hone the skills that will help me improve my job performance and grow as a person. Along with asking for feedback, looking for opportunities to learn new skills and hone the skills you already have shows you're holding yourself accountable for advancing your career. The goal of career advancement is a motivator for being accountable. This statement doesn't only bring into question whether an individual is willing to learn and grow, it also makes you think about whether you, as an organization, are offering your staff the necessary opportunities for development.

Questionnaire Two

Part of good management practices and accountability is performing 360° surveys. These are surveys where management gets feedback from employees about their own performance. Asking your employees these questions will give you an idea of how they feel management operates and how accountable they feel management is, but it can sometimes feel like a kick in the teeth. Nobody likes to be told they are underperforming in any area of their job, but good leadership accountability demands you get feedback and be open to accepting that feedback instead of getting defensive. Accountability is, in part, learning to handle negative feedback as being constructive so you can learn where you're falling short, solve problems, and come up with solutions to allow yourself to grow and do a better job.

Again, how the staff feels about management accountability has a direct impact on how they feel about their personal accountability within the organization and how motivated they are to be accountable themselves. As a manager of any sort, asking your employees to give you feedback means you are being accountable for your own actions and decisions to improve overall organizational accountability. You are showing your staff that you are prepared to take responsibility for growing the culture of accountability across the whole company by holding management accountable for leading by example.

The following questions are focused on key areas where accountability is often an issue irrespective of what kind of organization you run. Don't forget to answer these questions yourself to gain insight about the accountability in your workspace from your perspective. Let's get started.

Rating System:

1. The company struggles with this. Everybody knows it but nobody talks about it.

2. The company finds this a challenge. Everybody acknowledges it but nobody does anything about it.

3. This varies based on the specific situation or person involved.

4. This isn't a big problem within the company, but it happens more often than it should.

5. This is not a problem the company has, it never happens.

Question	Rating
Do you think leadership falls short of taking accountability for their actions? How short do you think these poor leadership practices fall?	

Question	Rating
Leadership isn't just about bossing employees around. Leadership means owning actions and responsibilities by getting and accepting feedback from staff to help them understand where others feel they're not quite up to snuff.	
Does the company have a clearly defined purpose, set of values, and a vision it's working towards with which all employees can be held accountable? How well or how poorly has the company relayed its purpose, values, and goals to employees?	
Discipline is one of the pillars that prop up accountability. Where does discipline come from? It comes from clear goals and values. Nobody can be expected to be disciplined about reaching goals if they don't know what the company values are, what its purpose is, or what its vision for the future is.	
How well or how poorly does the company engage in crucial communication with employees? Does management shy away from having potentially difficult performance conversations with employees or tackle them head-on?	

Question	Rating
Performance conversations with underachieving employees are difficult but they are crucial to organizational success and building personal accountability. Nobody's going to be encouraged to take accountability for their actions if they aren't being held accountable and people skirt around difficult conversations about lackluster performance.	
To what degree does management engage with staff? What is the level of personal communication with employees to make them feel like a valued asset? Does management keep an open channel of constant communication with employees or only engage with them when there is a problem?	
Leadership doesn't equate to tyranny. Leadership is about having influence and exerting that influence appropriately. However, people can't be influenced if leaders don't connect with them. Part of management's responsibilities is maintaining that connection with employees and holding themselves accountable for having regular interactions with staff.	
How much finger-pointing happens in the	

Question	Rating
company? What is the level of blame-shifting and excuse-making going on in the company as a whole, including management?	
Accountability means taking responsibility. It's easy to make excuses or point a finger at someone else to avoid holding yourself accountable or being held accountable for your role in the conflict or poor performance. These accountability avoidance tactics happen at all levels of the company.	
Is there a lack of follow-through in the company? Does management say they're going to do something and then not do it? Do the consequences of non-performance happen?	
Follow-through is an important factor for accountability. If management says they're going to do something but don't, they aren't holding themselves accountable for their lack of action. If expectations are set and consequences laid down for not meeting those expectations; not following through on the consequences diminishes accountability.	
Are expectations clearly communicated by	

Question	Rating
the company and management? Do you know what you're supposed to do and what successful results will look like? How well or how poorly does the company provide clear expectations for employees?	
There cannot be accountability if the expectations aren't clear and staff don't know what positive results look like. Without a clear direction, employees cannot be held accountable for actions that led to failure.	
How much lateral movement is there for under-performing employees? Does management or the company simply move under-achievers around from one position to another?	
Lateral movement of employees who consistently underperform doesn't encourage accountability. Instead, these employees learn that not taking accountability, making excuses, and continuing to underperform won't equate to real consequences and it's okay to just continue doing it.	
Are staff members that have been working at the company offered promotions based	

Question	Rating
on their tenure while more qualified employees are overlooked? How often does this practice take place?	
Promotion based on how long an employee has been working for the company doesn't promote accountability from that employee and doesn't encourage other employees to be accountable. After all, what's the point of holding themselves accountable and excelling if they're just going to be passed up for career-advancing promotions?	
Does the company have a rewards system that doesn't discriminate between results and how those results were achieved? Are employees who achieve good results through good behavior rewarded the same as those who achieve good results through disregarding the company's values and/or integrity? How generalized is the rewards system in the company?	
Rewarding the right thing encourages accountability whereas rewarding the wrong thing encourages bad behavior. Accountability is a combination of getting the results and acknowledging how those results are achieved. An employee achieving results through	

Question	Rating
unethical behavior has no reason to hold themselves accountable for using only ethical means for achieving goals.	

Scoring Guideline: The higher the score, the better the company-wide accountability. If you receive feedback that amounts to less than 31 points, you may want to take a closer look at management and company practices that can be tweaked to increase accountability.

Chapter 2:

The Power of Emotional

Intelligence and

Assertiveness

Assertiveness is an invaluable skill in both your personal and professional relationships and it's directly related to your emotional intelligence. Contrary to what the name may imply by using the word "intelligence," not having great emotional intelligence skills doesn't mean you're stupid, not by a long shot. Let's explore what emotional intelligence is, what assertiveness is, and how they relate to each other and accountability.

What Is Emotional Intelligence?

Emotional intelligence, or EI, is a skill we learn at a young age. It develops from birth and involves how we handle our emotions. Sometimes those skills aren't effectively learned as a child but that doesn't mean you can't hone your emotional intelligence as an adult. Emotionally intelligent people can:

- Identify the emotions they are feeling.

- Understand their emotions.

- Use emotion to interact with others.

- Manage and handle emotions, both positive and negative.

Emotion is a powerful thing, it has a hand to play in our relationships with others and even our relationship with ourselves. How we feel about something controls how we think about it and respond to it. For instance, a negative emotion often leads to a negative thought which, in turn, results in negative behavior. How do EI skills impact our lives?

- We can more effectively identify negative emotions, understand how they are helpful, and put them aside so they don't have a negative influence on how we perceive ourselves, others, and situations.

- We can identify what other people are feeling which gives us a better idea of how to best respond to them.

- We are able to manage and motivate ourselves to reach our goals and be successful in both our personal and professional lives.

Emotional Intelligence in Leadership

To be a great leader, one must have mastered emotional intelligence. A good manager has to sharpen their EI to improve communication with employees. Assertive communication about accountability will encourage staff to cultivate an attitude of accountability instead of pointing fingers, making excuses, or feeling animosity because they perceive their ego as being under attack when faced with a review of their performance. You will be in a better position to get what you want from your staff and motivate them to improve their performance by being accountable for their actions and the results they achieve.

Effective leaders use emotional intelligence to:

- Communicate and instill an organizational identity that is meaningful to everyone involved.

- Create goals that others buy into.

- Motivate others to get excited about their role in the company.

- Encourage individual and team flexibility to deal with changing situations.

- Create a positive and confident environment.

To understand how leaders use EI to do these things, we need to understand the pillars of emotional intelligence. Some people promote four pillars while others promote five. Let's go with five since that offers an even deeper insight as to how EI creates a good leader. These five pillars are:

- Self-awareness
- Social-awareness
- Self-regulation
- Empathy
- Motivation

Self-Awareness

Self-awareness is pretty self-explanatory. It means how aware you are of yourself, your emotions, how you think, how your emotions and thoughts affect your behavior, and how your behavior affects the behavior of others.

Social-Awareness

The term "social-awareness" refers to the awareness of others' verbal and non-verbal cues; our ability to "read the room" so to speak. This awareness allows you to observe others and adapt your interaction with them according to how you observe and perceive them. You're able to communicate and engage with employees and colleagues with empathy because you're trying to understand the emotions which motivate their behavior.

Self-Regulation

Emotionally intelligent leaders are able to recognize their emotions, what triggers those emotions, acknowledge how helpful or unhelpful their emotions are, and how to manage them. This is an incredibly important factor in communication, especially having those difficult performance chats in which you want to encourage others to be accountable.

Empathy

Empathy is putting yourself in someone else's shoes and it is a valuable skill for communicating with everyone including peers, management, and staff. Understanding others' perspectives, their emotions, and situations that may be affecting their emotions and behavior is vital for building an accountable team. It helps you solve problems more effectively by taking the other parties' feelings and perspectives into account and communicating your own side of the story better.

Motivation

Being able to motivate yourself allows you to be the best you can be and perform to the highest possible standards. It also encourages you to hold yourself accountable for your actions. Leaders influence through modeling what they want to see in others. If you are motivated and accountable, you will inspire your team to be as well and can motivate your staff with greater success.

Emotional Intelligence and Excuses

Excuses are made when you feel your ego is threatened. Low levels of emotional intelligence play a role in making excuses because you aren't able to accurately identify and understand emotions. You can't effectively challenge unhelpful thoughts. Your ability to regulate your emotions and thoughts to handle taking responsibility isn't great. You also aren't able to separate your sense of self from feelings of embarrassment or shame; you aren't able to say, "Okay, I messed up. I own my mistakes and the results of those mistakes; they are actions. My actions may be part of my representation but they do not wholly define me as a person."

When you can't separate your ego from your actions to accept accountability, you are likely to make excuses to protect that sense of self. Emotional intelligence can help you overcome the excuse habit. Instead of feeling your sense of self is being threatened, you are able to acknowledge faults and failures and look for solutions that will help you avoid the same behaviors, mistakes, and failures in the future. Developing your EI is key to moving away from excuses and instead, accept responsibility for your actions.

Mindfulness for Emotional Intelligence

Mindfulness is a state of being fully present in the now. Not only can mindfulness help you develop and hone your emotional intelligence, but the combination of both is a communication powerhouse. Mindfulness enhances your leadership skills by supporting two of the five pillars of emotional intelligence; self-awareness and social awareness.

Mindfulness and Self-Awareness

Being self-aware allows you to recognize emotions as you feel them, understand the ensuing thought, pick up on your physical and emotional cues, and determine how best to regulate your emotions. The good news is you inherently have the ability to be mindful; it's not a skill you have to learn. All you have to do is practice it to get better at it and eventually it will become second nature.

So, how do mindfulness and self-awareness tie in with accountability? Personal accountability has a lot to do with the emotions you experience and the thoughts you have. Taking responsibility for actions that failed and being held accountable for that is tough on the ego. After all, nobody likes having their faults, mistakes, or failures brought to light. It means you have to acknowledge you're not doing well or living up to expectations. You also have to deal with the embarrassment and that just feels awful. These emotions are uncomfortable to experience. By being mindful of the present and aware of what you're feeling, you can determine what it is you're feeling and the reciprocating thoughts.

Developing your emotional intelligence allows you to accept and experience those emotions for what they are and understand why they've cropped up. You can learn to identify the thoughts that accompany them and challenge those thoughts to stay grounded in the conversation. Being criticized may lead to thoughts like, "How dare you criticize me, you're not perfect yourself!" These types of thoughts are an emotional defense mechanism designed to protect your sense of self. They lead to excuses being made to justify your actions and their results. Being able to challenge them prevents those thoughts from becoming a runaway train that's taking you and your responding actions with it.

Self-awareness and focusing on the here and now allows you to handle difficult discussions with an employee you're holding accountable. Someone fobbing their actions and responsibilities off with excuses is frustrating, to say the least. You may become angry and escalate the conversation into a full-blown confrontation. While you're getting increasingly angrier, the other person is becoming more defensive and emotional. Eventually, this escalation to confrontation leads to a breakdown in communication and damages the relationship between you, as a leader, and your staff. Being present in the moment and aware of yourself, you can pick up on the physical effects of emotions before you realize you're experiencing them. You can stop the train, regulate your emotions, and deal with the difficult situation more effectively.

The combination of remaining self-aware and in the present also facilitates active listening. You remain in the conversation so you can take on board everything that is being said and the points being raised without instinctively forming responses in your head. Focusing on your own emotions and thoughts when you're being held accountable distracts you from really hearing what is being said to you, so you don't get the whole story.

Mindfulness and Social-Awareness

When it comes to leadership, mindfulness allows you to become aware of what others are feeling and encourages empathy. You are focused on the here and now, so you can pick up the non-verbal cues others are providing which give you an indication of how they're feeling. Picking up on this subtle information allows you to adapt your communication to make it more effective. It also gives you the ability to recognize when this crucial conversation is in jeopardy and the safety of honest, open, and safe communication is at risk.

Emotional Intelligence for Assertiveness

Assertiveness is the ability to communicate your emotions, thoughts, beliefs, and values openly and honestly without resorting to aggression or bullying. It also means you don't allow yourself to become a doormat for others and have your rights trampled over without standing up for yourself. Assertiveness is that sweet spot between passive and aggressive and it gets things done more effectively and efficiently than either of the other two communication styles.

The best leaders are assertive, but why is that? Why can't a good leader be one who rules with an iron fist? The simple answer is respect and influence. Tyrannical leaders don't garner respect. They rule with fear which is tenuous at best. Fearful followers bow down before a bully but they're quick to join a *coup d'etat* given the chance. When people respect you, you are able to exert real influence on them and they will be loyal, even defending you from attack. Instead of joining a revolt, they'll squash it before it even begins.

On the flipside, being a *laissez-faire* leader who prefers to be passive can make you look like you have no backbone. This opens the door to disrespect from your straff and may encourage your employees to walk all over you. You will find it impossible to rally your team behind a common purpose and hold them accountable.

When you take the reins and lead a team, it is vitally important to hit that sweet spot between being a pushover and being a dictator. You need to be assertive. Now let's find out how assertiveness depends on emotional intelligence.

Assertiveness: Self-Awareness

Assertive leaders are self-aware, identifying emotions that need managing before they get out of control. This is important during disagreements or when you're holding someone accountable. If you aren't aware of how your emotions are influencing your thoughts, communication, and reactions; you may well end up becoming aggressive or stepping back more passively. Neither aggression nor passiveness gets anything done effectively.

During crucial communication with someone about accountability, being too aggressive may lead to the interaction degenerating into an all-out verbal brawl. The only outcomes of that situation are disrespect, distrust, harboring grudges, and continued hostility. None of these are conducive to building a culture of accountability within your team.

Likewise, being able to identify feelings that lead to passive reactions can stop you from being walked all over by an employee who is making excuses and refusing to be held accountable. Constantly letting people off the hook does nothing but perpetuate a culture of refusal to be accountable.

The first step to being assertive is to identify emotions and understand why you are feeling them. The next step is managing your emotions, especially unhelpful ones.

Assertiveness: Self-Regulation

Aggressive leaders allow feelings of anger and frustration to best them. They don't pull punches and don't identify the anger and frustration as unhelpful in the situation. Instead, they run with their anger and allow it to churn up angry thoughts which lead to aggressive words and actions.

Passive leaders allow feelings of guilt, fear of being disliked, and avoidance of confrontation to run the show. Instead of expressing themselves firmly but respectfully, they tend to avoid confrontation or compensate for any potential hurt feelings with too much leniency.

Assertive leaders identify their emotions through self-awareness and then regulate those emotions. They determine which emotions are helpful and which are unhelpful in the particular situation they're addressing. They acknowledge the non-constructive nature of certain emotions and choose not to allow those emotions to run rampant, dictate their thoughts, or influence their actions. This ability to self-regulate their emotions is the key to handling accountability discussions.

Assertiveness: Social Awareness

Barking orders and dishing out harsh criticism doesn't require a whole lot of emotional intelligence. In fact, the lack of emotional intelligence is a prerequisite for that kind of leadership style, especially when it comes to social awareness. Dictators don't need to have awareness of those around them and how they think or feel. They only have to focus on how they are feeling and their thoughts.

Assertive leaders, on the other hand, have great social awareness. They're natural diplomats, taking into account the feelings, thoughts, and situations of others at all times. Notice I've said "taking into account." Assertive leaders listen to others, consider their feelings, opinions, and rights, and make informed decisions. That's not to say others will always get their way because they've given their opinion. An assertive leader also won't let someone off the hook simply because they understand what the other person is feeling or going through. They will, however, give genuine consideration to what people say and their actions are based on fairness. Their awareness and consideration of others in a social context is part of what makes great leaders so successful.

Assertiveness: Empathy

Being empathetic and being assertive may seem like trying to fit two opposing teams into one camp. How can you be empathetic and assertive at the same time?

The trick is to understand that they are not opponents, they are playing for the same team. The disconnect between empathy and assertiveness is the social assumption that being empathetic means being a pushover. People think you can't put yourself in someone else's position and see their perspective without losing sight of your own and automatically bowing down to their wants, needs, opinions, or excuses. The problem with that way of thinking is that it's neither true nor helpful.

Good leaders are able to be empathetic and assertive at the same time. They can listen with empathy, see things from another's perspective, and take that person's feelings and thoughts into account while still standing firmly by their decisions, opinions, and values. Empathy is a vital part of emotional intelligence. Emotional intelligence is integral to assertiveness. So, it stands to reason that being empathetic is part of being an assertive leader.

Aggressive leaders lack empathy. They want what they want and they want it done now. Passive leaders have too much empathy and allow themselves to be swayed by feeling bad for other people. An assertive leader will hear someone out, look at all the facts, and adjust their communication, expectations, and actions according to what they perceive to be the best path to take for the best results.

Emotional Intelligence Self-Assessment

Testing your emotional intelligence can help you figure out where you stand on the accountability scale and whether you need to work at improving your EI.

Instructions:

Below are five tables, each addressing a different component of emotional intelligence, and each with a series of questions. Assign each one a rating and tally up your score at the end to get a better idea of how emotionally intelligent you are in that area of EI.

Important note: This self-assessment exercise is not an accurate psychological test. The results are only a guideline to help you get an idea of what your level of emotional intelligence is.

Rating System:
1. Not at all
2. Rarely
3. Sometimes/half the time
4. Often
5. Very often/always

Self-Awareness Questions	Rating
Do you realize you're losing your temper immediately when it happens?	
When you're stressed out, do you recognize that you're feeling stressed?	
Do you know when you are happy?	
Do you know what makes you happy?	
Are you aware of it when you are being or feeling emotional?	
When you are being unreasonable, are you always aware of it?	
Can you pinpoint the reasons for anxious feelings?	
Is it important to you to be aware of your emotions all the time?	
If someone has annoyed or upset you, are you aware of it?	
Are you able to let go of anger quickly?	

Total Score	

Self-Regulation Questions	Rating
Can you quickly and easily reframe negative situations to view them differently?	
Are you a person who avoids showing emotion or who doesn't "wear their heart on their sleeve"?	
Are you a person who avoids emotional outbursts toward other people?	
Are you someone that others find difficult to read or tell what your mood is?	
Are you the kind of person who isn't irritated by difficult people?	
Are you a person who leaves work stress behind when you go home, not allowing it to affect you once you leave?	
Can you make the deliberate decision to change your mood or mental state?	
Are you someone who doesn't worry much	

Self-Regulation Questions	Rating
about life and work?	
Do others not really know how you feel about situations?	
When necessary, are you able to suppress your emotions?	
Total Score	

Motivation Questions	Rating
Can you always motivate yourself to face difficult tasks?	
Are your deadlines always met?	
Are you able to prioritize tasks and get them done?	
Are you someone who doesn't beat around the bush?	
Are you a person who doesn't waste time?	

Motivation Questions	Rating
Are you someone who prefers to skip small immediate gratification and hold out for something bigger and better down the line?	
Are you a believer in getting the hardest work out of the way first?	
Are you able to motivate yourself, even when you aren't feeling great?	
Do you prefer to get things done instead of procrastinating?	
Has motivation played a pivotal role in your success?	
Total Score	

Empathy Questions	Rating
Can you always see things from someone else's perspective?	
When someone isn't happy with you, can you pick up on it?	

Empathy Questions	Rating
Can you empathize with the problems of others?	
If there is discord within a team and the members aren't getting along, can you pick up on it?	
Do you believe that others are simply "different" as opposed to "difficult"?	
When people are being "difficult," can you generally understand why?	
When others are offended by your actions, can you understand why?	
If you are being unreasonable, can you understand why?	
Are you able to only sometimes see things from another person's viewpoint?	
When there are disagreements, can you always clearly see the reasons behind them?	
Total Score	

Social Skills Questions	Rating
Do you actively listen to others without interruptions or losing interest?	
Are you good at mingling with and adapting to a variety of different people?	
Are you someone who doesn't interrupt the conversations of others?	
Do you find other people extremely interesting?	
Is your job only interesting if you are surrounded by a variety of people in your workspace?	
Do you enjoy meeting new people and finding out what makes them who they are?	
When faced with difficult people, do you view the situation as just a challenge to yourself to bring them around?	
Do you enjoy finding out what others hold as important by asking them questions?	
When working with others, do you strive to build good relationships with them?	

Social Skills Questions	Rating
When there are differences between others and yourself, are you good at making amends?	
Total Score	

Once you have tallied up all your scores for the individual sections, use the scoring guide below to see how you stack up in each category.

10-17: You need to put in the work needed to develop this area of your emotional intelligence.

18-34: This area of your emotional intelligence could do with some attention.

35-50: This area of your emotional intelligence is one of your strengths.

Assertiveness Self-Assessment

You may already have a good idea of how assertive you are, and that's great. However, your perception of your own assertiveness comes from a place of subjectivity. You aren't necessarily looking at yourself and your level of assertiveness from an objective point of view. Answer the following questions honestly and make notes of your answers to use against the scoring guide afterward.

1. Are you clear and direct when you address people or a situation?

2. Do you make direct eye contact with people when speaking to them?

3. Do you sit or stand up straight instead of slouching?

4. Are you comfortable being around other people?

5. When you need clarification, are you confident to ask questions?

6. Can you express your emotions effectively?

7. Are you comfortable saying "no" to others?

8. If you are blamed for something that isn't your fault, do you stand up for yourself?

9. If you disagree with an opinion or situation, do you speak your mind?

10. Do you speak confidently to others?

These are all yes-no questions. Count how many questions you answered with "no" to see how your assertiveness stacks up.

-   0-3: You don't have much difficulty in asserting yourself, your needs, or your wants.

- 4-6: You experience some difficulty with assertiveness.

- 7-10: Your assertiveness needs some serious work to stop you from being a pushover.

Another way to assess your assertiveness and help you find the correct balance for handling situations assertively is to think about a past scenario. Think of a personal experience to make the exercise more effective and using a recent occurrence will allow you to recall more detail. Think about what happened and consider aggressive, passive, and assertive responses to the situation. Then think about what your actual response was and compare it to the passive, aggressive, and assertive response suggestions.

For example:

What happened?	A colleague asked me to take over some of their responsibilities.
What would an aggressive response be?	"No, handle your own work instead of trying to fob it off on someone else!"
What would a passive response be?	"Yes, what do you want me to do?"
What would an assertive	"I have a policy of not

response be?	taking over other's responsibilities without following the proper chain of command."
What was your actual response?	"Okay, we can talk about it."

As you can see, the actual response wasn't passive or aggressive, it was a reasonable response if you had the knowledge, skills, resources, and time to help your colleague out. However, assertiveness isn't just about saying yes or no. It's also about protecting your principles and values. As far as accountability is concerned, the response was a veritable minefield. Why? You are taking accountability for responsibilities that were not given to you in the first place. Simply accepting information from your colleague could leave you with an incomplete picture of what, exactly, is expected and what the outcomes should be. You are setting yourself up for not meeting expectations, even if they weren't officially given to you originally, and for possibly failing or not doing the job correctly. In the end, you could end up getting flack for something you shouldn't be held accountable for but which you committed to without ensuring you could be held accountable but that's not where the story ends. You are sabotaging your personal accountability as well. You are holding yourself accountable for your actions and part of that accountability is following the due processes, officially accepting the responsibility, and ensuring you are clear on what is expected.

Improving Emotional Intelligence

Improving your emotional intelligence may help you become more assertive and both be accountable and hold others accountable. Here are some ways you can build up your emotional intelligence in the different categories we've just been exploring.

Use the following exercise daily to help you identify what emotions you felt in a specific situation or throughout the day. By doing this exercise over several days or weeks, you will notice patterns to help you connect the dots between your emotions and specific situations or people. You will also be able to see trends in how often you feel certain emotions and even how different moods affect how you feel about the same thing. You will also be challenging yourself to view and think about things differently and practice empathy.

Situation Specific:

After a situation where negative feelings crop up, write down the following:

- **The Situation:** What happened? Who were you with? What is your relationship with that person?

- **Emotions:** What emotions were you feeling before the situation happened? What emotions did you feel during the situation? Identify and name the emotions. Circle or highlight the strongest emotion.

- **Thoughts:** What thoughts popped up in relation to the situation and how you were feeling. Circle or highlight the most dominating thought.

- **The Why:** Try to understand and write down why you felt the strongest emotion and why the dominant thought arose.

- **The How:** How did you respond to the situation, your emotions, and your thoughts?

- **What Next:** Could you view the situation differently? How could you see it from a different perspective?

- **Empathize:** Put the shoe on the other foot. How would you have felt if you were in the other person's position?

- **Next Step:** Could you have handled the situation differently? How can you better deal with the same situation, or a similar one, in the future?

Making notes of your emotional responses and the corresponding thoughts and actions in response to a specific situation may help you:

- Gain a deeper insight into your emotions.

- Observe how feelings prior to a situation can affect your emotions, thoughts, and reactions during it.

- Determine what triggers your emotions.

- Understand why your emotions and thoughts arise.

- See things from the other person's perspective.

- Find more effective ways of managing your emotions and thoughts.

- Find more constructive ways to handle difficult situations for a more positive outcome.

By practicing this exercise regularly, your emotional intelligence grows as you become more aware of your own emotions and thoughts. You're also teaching yourself to at least try to see things from another point of view and engage in problem-solving to find different ways to handle situations more effectively.

Throughout the Day:

Even if something upsetting or frustrating didn't happen, reflect on your day. Make notes of the following:

- **Mood:** What was your mood like? Did it fluctuate?

- **Emotions:** What emotions do you recall feeling? Name the emotions specifically and label them as positive or negative.

- **Assessment:** Examine the emotions. Try to determine why you felt the emotions you did throughout the day.

Resist the temptation to replay negative situations and brood over them. Avoid trying to label your emotions as right or wrong. This exercise is simply to bring your attention to your emotions and create awareness. Notice how many positive and negative emotions you felt during the day. Determine which emotions had the greatest impact on you during the day.

Improving Assertiveness

Improving your assertiveness ties in with improving your emotional intelligence. You can start improving both at the same time. I'm going to give you some tips for improving your assertiveness starting today.

Identify, Challenge, and Change Unhelpful Thoughts

The first step to beefing up your assertiveness is to change the way you think. Identifying unhelpful thoughts is a process that requires self-awareness. It's not always possible to challenge and change unhelpful thoughts when you are in the middle of a situation but you can reflect on them afterward and then apply your findings to future situations. After you've had an experience where you lacked assertiveness, use the following questions as a guideline for improvement. This is especially effective for situations where you weren't able to turn down a request.

What happened? Where were you? Who were you with?	A friend you aren't particularly close to asked to borrow some money from you while you were out with several other friends.
What feelings, thoughts, and beliefs made you say "yes"?	You felt embarrassed to say no in front of your friends. You believed you would be seen as selfish or rude. You thought you may lose favor with your friends if you refused.

Before moving on to the next step, think about the following:

- When you say "no," you aren't rejecting the person, only their request.
- People have the right to make requests of you and you have the right to refuse those requests.
- You are always in control of your own decisions. Saying "yes" to one thing could mean saying "no" to another. (In this example, agreeing to lend a friend money may be saying no to your personal policy of not lending money to friends which means you're going against your own values.)
- Declining a request now doesn't mean that person can never make another request ever again.
- If you communicate your feelings openly and freely, you are giving the other person the opportunity and encouragement to do the same.

Taking the above into consideration, how can you challenge the thoughts, feelings, and beliefs that made you agree? What helpful thoughts could you replace them with to empower you to say no in the future?	Remind yourself of your principles and values. Challenge the embarrassment by acknowledging that there is nothing wrong with saying no. You cannot control what others think about you. Your friends should respect your values.

You can apply this exercise to a variety of scenarios to help identify and challenge unhelpful thoughts that don't support assertiveness.

Chapter 3:

Confronting Accountability:

The Preparation

Holding others accountable for their actions, whether in your personal or professional life, is never easy. It's one of those difficult conversations that you can't just jump into. You need to prepare for this type of crucial communication and in this chapter, we're going to explore how to properly prepare for confronting accountability.

Should Someone be Confronted?

This is the crux of the matter. When dealing with personal situations, just because someone has failed to be accountable for their actions doesn't mean confrontation is necessary. However, in the workplace, accountability problems should always be addressed to be consistent and to help employees make sure it doesn't happen again. So, this question is really aimed at your personal relationships outside of the workplace.

Ask yourself the following questions to decide whether or not someone really should be confronted about not taking accountability.

Does it keep bothering me? Sometimes it's useful to take some time to decide whether or not it will continue to bother you and a confrontation is really needed.

How often does it happen? If this is someone's first offense, bringing it up may not be necessary. Letting a lack of accountability slide once may not be a terrible thing. After all, you don't know if it'll happen again. However, if it's happened multiple times before, it's probably time to bring it up and speak your mind.

How serious is the situation? Some instances of not taking accountability aren't so serious while other times it can be very serious. Considering the consequences of the situation can help decide if it's worth discussing.

Has it hurt your relationship? If the relationship has changed and your behavior toward that person has become more passive-aggressive, it's probably a good idea to have that difficult conversation.

What will be the outcome of the confrontation? What do you think will happen if you don't discuss the situation? What do you think will happen if you do have that conversation? This if-then conundrum is the reason you should take some time to decide whether the discussion is necessary and decide if the relationship has been hurt by the situation.

Pick the Right Problem

Dealing with accountability may seem simple. After all, the person is just not holding themselves accountable for their actions so it's just about addressing their lack of accountability, right? Not really. The umbrella may be accountability but there may be more going on that needs to be addressed. For instance, an employee may be missing deadlines and producing poor quality work but may also have an attitude problem causing tension between coworkers. Both problems revolve around accountability. How an employee behaves and their attitude requires them to be held accountable just as much as missed deadlines and poor work quality. However, they are two separate issues and shouldn't be thrown together in a single meeting.

To make the message stick, you need to pick one topic to address for a meeting. Combining too many areas of discussion in one conversation turns it into a tossed salad where everything gets jumbled up. This causes confusion and your message gets lost. You need to pick one problem and focus only on that problem. Which of the two in the example above is the most critical to address? Prioritize the problems you see with someone's accountability and tackle them separately in a series of meetings, starting with the most urgent.

Gather Your Evidence

Whether you're confronting a friend or an employee, you cannot go into a discussion about accountability unless you have your ducks in a row and evidence prepared. Evidence should be fair and, if possible, based on your observations and not someone else's. That isn't always possible, but using your personal observations cuts out any finger-pointing and minimizes friction between people. The minute you bring in a scenario of he said-she said, the person you're dealing with may feel like they are being attacked and victimized by others and could go on the defensive. You could also face a situation of retaliation and "but so-and-so does such-and-such and gets away with it!"

Having hard evidence is the best-case scenario. Incontestable proof of the person's lack of accountability gives them no room for accusing you of being unfair. You can also keep the discussion on track more easily and make your points clearer.

Define the Problem

Holding someone accountable is all about communication. You can learn all about the different types of communication and how to communicate effectively in my other book, *Crucial Communication*, but

I will now explain why communication is crucial for accountability.

When there is a lack of accountability, it has to be made clear what is happening that indicates that lack. Before you can begin to tackle the problem, you need a clear definition of it.

Let's revisit that homework example we got to know so well in chapter one to illustrate defining the problem.

- **What is the actual problem?** Homework not completed on time is a missed deadline.

- **What is the action or lack of action causing the problem?** Procrastination, miscommunication, misaligned priorities, a low level of motivation, disinterest. All of these are possible reasons for the problem. If you know what the reason behind the problem is, use it as part of the definition of the issue being addressed.

- **Where is the problem occurring?** At home and at school are the only two locations for this particular example. However, when it comes to holding someone accountable for their work behavior, it could be the office, at home (if the person works remotely), at a work function, at a client's premises.

- **When did the problem happen?** Times and dates provide backup evidence to support your case. For example, homework was not completed on Tuesday afternoon for it to be handed in on Wednesday morning.

- **Who was involved?** My trusty homework example isn't necessarily the best example for this question. The student in question would be the person involved. However, putting it into a teamwork assignment example, there may be other students involved who are affected by one person's lack of accountability. In the workplace, a conflict between coworkers could be used as an example in which case, the coworkers involved would be named.

All of this information helps you define the problem to the fullest possible extent. Why is defining the problem so important? You cannot address an issue if you don't provide a clear explanation of what it is. This is why communication is vital for accountability. Clarity leaves no room for misunderstandings which could disrupt the progress of the resolution.

Understand the Problem

Now that you have defined the problem as clearly as you can, it's time to really understand it. You cannot help employees learn and grow if you don't understand the problem yourself. In management, it's all too easy to forget that part of your job is to facilitate employee growth. Many people fall into the trap of thinking they are only there to make sure staff get the job done when that is only one part of a leader's job description. If there is an issue that needs to be addressed, simply confronting the person isn't where the resolution process ends. It's now up to both of you to come up with possible ways to fix the situation and get your employee back on the right track.

Avoid Negative Thinking

You need to stay open-minded when tackling a problem. Negative thinking is the arch-nemesis of open-mindedness. There are several negative thinking styles you need to watch out for.

Over-generalization: Avoid looking at the problem and seeing everything about the employee as a problem or suggesting that they always have this issue and always will. Even if this is not the first time the issue is being addressed, remain positive and stick to the facts. Avoid using the term "always;" "You're always late" or "You always miss deadlines" and replace them with factual information such as "You have been late for work five times this month" or "You have missed the deadlines on your last three projects."

Jumping to conclusions: Assumptions make a fool of anybody. Jumping to conclusions if you don't have all the facts to make an informed decision is a terrible way to approach a problem. You are not only risking making yourself look bad and losing the respect of your staff,you are also giving your employees the impression you think badly of them. Unfortunately, most of the time when we jump to conclusions in these kinds of situations it's because we catastrophize and go from "There is a problem" to "This is the worst possible thing ever."

Fortune telling: Trying to predict how your employee will react to the confrontation about their lack of accountability isn't going to help you focus on the problem at hand and find solutions. You aren't a mind reader and you cannot foresee the future so resist the temptation to try to predict how things will turn out.

Magnifying: Avoid making mountains out of molehills. You must approach the problem with an appropriate level of concern and consequence that's proportionate to how severe the problem is.

Perfectionism: "Should and must" thinking is more applicable to dealing with accountability in your personal life but it can also complicate things and close your mind off in a professional setting. This type of thinking projects your subjective expectations onto others. Thinking that someone "should" know something, for instance, opens up a can of misunderstanding worms. Believing that someone "must" see things from your perspective isn't going to make that happen. Perfectionism also has a hand to play in setting unrealistic goals and expectations. For instance, expecting that an employee should know something doesn't help either of you understand the problem. Perhaps the problem has arisen from miscommunication you didn't know was happening.

Factual, Realistic, and Objective

It can be easy to lean toward emotional opinions and realistic objectivity. Emotions come into play in every aspect of our lives. However, when dealing with accountability in interpersonal relationships, emotions and subjectivity must be put aside. Emotions can cloud your judgment and distort your perception of situations. These feelings can stem from personal circumstances in your life and what you are going through or they can come from an emotional connection to the situation. It is important to keep perspective. How do you do this?

Collect and look at the facts. Facts can be found in observations and performance metrics. When it comes to using observations, it is vital that you don't take the opinions of others into account. Wherever possible, you need to use your own observations of the situation. You also need to use objective observations. Assumption and prediction have no place in considering what has happened or why.

Look at the situation realistically. What are the realistic expectations for the person you are dealing with? Are your expectations too high? Does the person have the resources to meet your expectations? These are all things you need to consider when deciding whether you are taking a realistic approach to understand the problem.

Stay objective. This means distancing yourself from your emotions. What if you don't like the person you are holding accountable? Well, that doesn't matter. You cannot allow your personal feelings to distort your perception of the situation and judge the lack of accountability too harshly.

Determine and Define the Repercussions

A lack of accountability naturally comes with repercussions. To understand the extent of the problem, you need to look at the consequences. All forms of refusing to be accountable should be addressed, yes, but the severity of the consequences should be proportionate. They form part of the problem and need to be brought up when holding someone accountable for their actions. These repercussions will also determine what the consequences for the person in question should be. If a deadline was missed but the result of that wasn't critical, the consequences shouldn't be as harsh as if the missed deadline caused the company a lot of trouble. To understand the consequences of a lack of accountability, consider who or what was affected, how, and to what extent.

Make Sure There are Policies

As part of your preparation, ensure there are company policies in place that require the person to take accountability for their actions. Make sure these policies are readily available to all employees, should they want to jog their memory, and that they are made aware of them in the first place. If there aren't policies that speak to the particular problem, the employee can't be held accountable or they may call you out for being unfair or victimizing.

What Is Wanted?

Finding a solution seems to be an obvious part of the process of creating accountability but it's not where you should be starting. When someone wants to find a solution, there is an underlying need or want that is motivating them to find that solution. What does the person you're confronting want from finding a way to overcome their accountability issues? The desire to solve the problem has to have an advantage for them. There's no motivation to find a solution and stick with it if there's no advantage. You can also consider what you and the other person don't want to have happen as a result of their lack of accountability. This provides further insight into what solutions may get you both what you want and avoid what you don't want.

It's the typical case of "What's in it for me?" You discover the direction your problem-solving should go in when you understand what will motivate them to fix the issue. This makes coming to a win-win solution so much easier.

Keep It Concise

There is nothing more confusing than rambling on. Long-winded explanations distract you and your employee from the points you are trying to get across;the message you are trying to drive home gets lost. You also risk losing their attention if they can't keep up and their mind starts wandering because there's too much waffle in between the important bits.

Work your way through the steps I've just listed in preparing for tackling the absence of accountability. Write down:

- What the problem is.

- What evidence supports the need for the discussion.

- The detailed definition of the problem.

- The repercussions the lack of accountability has for the company and the individual.

- Any policies the company has in place that make the discussion warranted.

- What you, as the manager, want to see happen.

Once you have all of those points jotted down, you can figure out how to state your case as clearly and concisely as possible. If you can, try to narrow it down to two or three sentences to avoid confusion and the point of the discussion falling on deaf ears because your employee has lost interest.

For example:

- Homework was not completed.

- This is supported by it not being handed in on time.

- Defining the problem: Homework was not completed on Tuesday to be handed in on Wednesday. The reason behind it seems to be a lack of interest/motivation as previously observed inside the classroom. This occurred outside of the school. The person involved in the repercussions is the student.

- The consequence of the action is poor grades.

- The student knows s/he is expected to do the homework which has been made clear multiple times.

- As the teacher, you don't want to see the student get poor grades as it will affect their future.

Now it's time to compose that concise statement.

"You did not complete your homework on Tuesday and it wasn't handed in on time on Wednesday. You've previously been disinterested in the classroom and your grades are suffering. You know you are expected to do the homework. I don't want to see you fail the class and have that affect your future."

Okay, so that's four sentences, but you get the idea. The statement is short and sweet and gets straight to the point. You are not leaving any chance of miscommunication. This statement should be rehearsed so that when you deliver it, you know exactly what you want to say but don't want to rattle it off like a robot.

Chapter 4:

Confronting Accountability:

The Discussion

After you've carefully prepared for tackling someone's lack of accountability, it's time to have that discussion. These difficult conversations are never easy or fun and that goes for all parties involved. However, no matter how uncomfortable it is; when you're in a leadership position, you just have to suck it up and get it done. Remember, letting an absence of accountability slide only sets a team up for disgruntled employees and a breakdown in the culture of accountability you want to foster. In personal relationships, not addressing the issue may lead to resentment and anger building up and festering, poisoning your relationship from the inside.

Pick the Right Time

You should always address accountability issues as soon as possible after they make themselves known. The sooner you do it, the sooner potential consequences are stopped. In a personal capacity, it stops animosity from building up and changing your behavior which could damage the relationship. In a professional capacity, it can affect the company's performance and revenue, create a disconnect between team members or departments, and it could even affect the company's image and reputation. So, the sooner the better, but it's also important to pick the right time.

Timing is a huge factor for addressing accountability problems. Some issues need to be addressed the same day, especially if severe consequences are the result. Other issues can wait a few days, a week, or even longer. There are a few things to take into account when deciding when to confront someone about a lack of accountability. Are they going through a significantly tough time in their personal lives which could be affecting their performance? Everybody says you shouldn't allow your personal circumstances to affect your work, but there may be some exceptions to that rule. Something like the death or severe illness of a close family member takes a big toll on someone's mental and physical health, but something like a relationship breakup may not warrant the same kind of delay. If you know someone's personal circumstances are dire and are probably the cause of the problem, perhaps it's better to wait a while before having that talk. This is especially true if that person hasn't got a track record of accountability issues.

Choose the Right Environment

Pick an environment for the conversation that is conducive to creating a sense of safety for the person in question. An environment they feel threatened in will leave them feeling on edge, defensive, and unreceptive. This kind of uneasy feeling will possibly lead to the talk being unsuccessful.

For personal relationships, choose a place that feels safe for both of you. Somewhere away from any emotional connection to the environment that you're in. This helps disconnect your emotions from the discussion so you're calmer and more willing to engage.

For workplace conflict resolution, choosing an environment that makes the employee feel safe may not be possible. Your office might intimidate your staff because it is a place of power, and this is especially true of timid or passive employees. Sometimes, no matter how approachable you are as a manager, there are just those employees that will feel intimidated by anyone above them. If your office seems like it may feel threatening to an employee, try another space, such as the boardroom or even the break room between staff breaks when it's empty.

Important note: Never confront a staff member in the middle of an open office where all their teammates and other staff are watching and listening in. This humiliating experience is likely to put them on the back foot and distract them from really hearing you out. The same goes for personal relationships. Confronting someone in front of their friends or family will be embarrassing which could degenerate the conversation into an all-out fight.

Have a Witness Present

I know I just said not to confront someone publicly but that doesn't mean someone can't be present as a witness. This is especially useful in workplace discussions. The employee you are addressing may still feel a little embarrassed at their accountability faults being pointed out in front of someone else, yes. However, having a witness present ensures that both you and the person you're talking to are on their best behavior. There is also someone who can back up your side of the story if the employee goes to HR and complains about unfairness or victimization. It won't always be possible to have a witness present but it's not a bad idea for times when it is possible.

Document the Meeting

In the workplace, if you don't record crucial interactions with staff, you don't have a leg to stand on if it happens again. Even verbal warnings can be recorded. You don't necessarily have to have minutes taken for one-on-one meetings, but you should at least have the employee sign a statement that provides details such as the date of the meeting and what was discussed.

Engage Mindfully

In *Crucial Communication*, I discuss how to have difficult discussions in great depth and walk you through having those talks step-by-step. For addressing accountability problems, I'll touch briefly on how to use mindful communication to engage employees and personal relationships for a successful outcome.

Listen Actively

I touched on active listening in Chapter 2. It's the skill of being able to listen to someone else without interrupting, forming responses in your head while they're talking, or letting your thoughts run away with you. Active listening means you are fully present and completely engaged with the other person. Mastering this skill will help your communication with others to no end.

Don't Allow Interruptions

Just because you employ active listening doesn't mean the other person will. When someone is trying to defend and justify their actions, they are prone to interrupting you while you're speaking. If this happens, gently and respectfully remind them to allow you to finish before saying their piece. Allowing interruptions undermines your assertiveness and shows others that they can invalidate your contribution by talking over you.

Mind Your Tone

Keep your tone even and calm to help the other person feel safe. Using a reassuring tone makes them feel less threatened which may improve their receptiveness to your message.

Watch Your Words

Choosing the right words is a skill all assertive leaders must hone. Words may have different connotations for different people. Choosing the right words helps get your message across effectively and helps avoid misunderstandings.

Steer Clear of Emotional Language in the Workplace

When confronting an employee about their accountability, steer clear of language and statements that describe how you feel. Using feeling statements turns the focus of the talk from the accountability problem to you, and you don't want that. You want to make sure they don't get the impression it's a problem with you personally, but rather that it's a team or company problem. Try to avoid making "I" statements; they single you out as the one who has a problem with the staff member's actions. You must also be mindful to not use "you" statements at the same time. "You" statements can often make a serious discussion feel like an attack for the person being dealt with. Instead, opt for "we" and "the company" statements. This puts the focus on the company's expectations and needs and makes the discussion feel less threatening or attacking and more neutral.

For example, use a statement like "You're turning up late for work more regularly lately has been noticeable" instead of "I've noticed you are turning up late for work more regularly lately." See how the first statement feels less attacking and shifts the focus from you and the person in question to their behavior?

Use "I" Statements for Personal Confrontations

Unlike workplace accountability issues, having this kind of difficult conversation in a personal relationship requires an expression of your own feelings about what is happening. When confronting someone in a personal capacity, use statements like "I feel...when you..." instead of "You make me...because you..." This shifts the focus from the person to how you feel and the action that makes you feel that way. The shift tells the person it's not them, personally, that's the problem but rather their actions.

Use "Yes, and..." Statements

"Yes, and" statements have been used in improv comedy as a staple for ages, but how does it make its way into your personal and professional life? Even more importantly, why would you want to say "yes" to something you want to say "no" to? To understand how these statements work, you need to break them down.

"Yes" is an affirmation. It doesn't necessarily mean you are agreeing with something you in fact disagree with; you are simply using it to affirm that you have heard and understood what the other person is saying to you. That is the tricky part to wrap your mind around. It's been indoctrinated into us that "yes" means agreeing with whatever is being said or agreeing to whatever is being asked of you. When using "Yes, and" statements, that isn't the case. After all, you can't just go around agreeing with everything and anything anybody says all the time, can you? However, you can let the person know you have received the message they are trying to get across to you. Combine that with repeating back their message and you are confirming that you were actively listening and empathizing.

Let's go back to that trusty homework example I like to use. Imagine yourself in the teacher's position and you are dealing with a student who has failed to complete and turn in their homework. For the sake of this version, let's say the student was representing the school in an important sports match the afternoon before and ran out of time to do the homework. It's not possible to let them off the hook because of extracurricular activities because that would be setting a bad precedent. You could approach the situation with "yes" by saying, "Yes, I hear you were representing the school in a sports match." Do you see how you haven't agreed to anything aside from acknowledging they were playing sport?

Now that we have the "yes" part down, it's time to move on to the "and" part. The "and" is an ingenious way of connecting your acknowledgment of what the person says with a decline to meet their request or agree with a statement. It is the single most powerful connector you can use in business and in your personal life.

Back to the example to illustrate just how it fits in before we get to the part about why "and" is better than "but" because I know you're wondering about the switcheroo. As the teacher, it would not be fair to other students to allow students with extracurricular activities to shirk their homework responsibilities. Not doing the homework or not completing it is just not going to happen. Your response would look something like this, "Yes, I hear you were representing the school in a sports match, and it's not fair to let you off the hook for not finishing your homework because of extracurricular activities."

What you've done by using "and" is acknowledge their message and relay that it's not possible to give them what they want. However, unlike using "but," "and" is a conversation opener, not a conversation closer. When you use "but" you are making the refusal a priority and not giving the person and yourself the opportunity to explore other options. The term "but" squashes any chance of problem-solving to find a win-win solution.

Understand Emotional Reactions

The situation is likely to be emotionally charged whenever you sit down to have a difficult conversation with someone. It is vitally important to remain both self-aware and socially aware. You are able to identify, understand, monitor, and self-regulate your own emotions with self-awareness. Social awareness, on the other hand, allows you to pick up on how the other person is reacting to what you're discussing. You can detect when a conversation is at risk of escalating into an emotional ticking time bomb. Understanding the emotional responses of others helps you remain calm, even if they are getting upset. You can adapt your communication to lead the conversation back to safety. To find out more about how to manage the safety of a critical conversation, refer to *Crucial Communication* where I explore the topic in full detail.

Get To the Root of the Problem

In the previous chapter, I discussed the importance of understanding the problem. You can speculate where the problem comes from while preparing for a critical discussion about a lack of accountability. You can use your observations as a starting point but you can't be 100% sure; at that point, it's all still guesswork. Now that you've sat the person down, here's your chance to hear their side of the story and really dig deeper.

It can be very tempting to want to make yourself heard above and beyond what the other person has to say, especially in a management position. After all, you're the boss, right? Yes, you are the boss. However, an assertive boss doesn't feel like they have to interrupt someone else while they're speaking, or talk over them. Their main focus isn't on making sure their point of view is understood irrespective of what others have to say. An assertive leader wants to listen, gather as much information as they can, and get a better idea of what is in fact going on. Avoid falling into the "My point is the one that matters so you have to listen to me more than I have to listen to you" trap, as it'll get you nowhere.

Understanding the reason for an accountability problem is the only way to truly come to a resolution that will stick. When the other person feels heard and valued, they are more likely to maintain open communication. They feel that you see them as more than just another cog in the company wheel and they are likely to be more open to and receptive toward compromising and working together to find a win-win solution. Getting to the bottom of the issue also opens the door to creative problem-solving. Someone else may come up with an idea you hadn't thought about. You never know, maybe your guess about the cause is way off, and therefore the solution you came up with is completely wrong for the situation.

Don't Point Fingers or Allow Finger Pointing

Let's take a moment to talk about pointing fingers. We've discussed it in relation to your personal accountability, now I'm going to put it into the context of dealing with someone else's accountability problems. The success of critical communication is creating a safe space to talk openly about issues someone may be having. Aggressively blaming a person shuts down the communication in a heartbeat and turns finding a solution into an impossible mission. Consider this, if you were in the other person's position, would you want to be blamed to the exclusion of what you have to say? The same goes for allowing someone to point fingers and lay blame everywhere else. When finger-pointing begins, it's important to gently guide the spotlight back onto the person in question. Allowing finger-pointing makes room for excuses to begin creeping in, and once you allow excuses to start and begin accepting those excuses it's all downhill from there.

Avoid Trying to Mind-Read

Have you ever found yourself trying to anticipate what someone is thinking and what they're going to say? That's called mind-reading. You are convincing yourself of what someone else is thinking. It's a form of assumption and it's all based on your own, subjective point of view. The truth is, you can't possibly know what another person is thinking. The only person who knows that is them. Mind-reading leads to jumping to conclusions which threatens communication as a whole. You are going to make the other person feel undermined, attacked, and like you have no interest in their experience or perspective of the situation. It's very tempting, I know. It may even be habitual because we all do it so often, but it is a habit we must break.

Give Not into the Temptation to Argue

Arguing; you hear the word often and have probably used it more times than you can remember. It's something people do often. We bicker and fight amongst ourselves without ever realizing how damaging it is to our interpersonal relationships. You probably also don't realize how strongly it points to a lack of positive communication, conflict management, and problem-solving skills. It also tells the world you're not an assertive person. In short, arguing is the opposite of what you want to achieve when trying to find a way to improve accountability.

Why do we argue, though? The biggest reason discussions degenerate into arguments is ego. As I mentioned earlier, there's this psychological defense mechanism that kicks in when you feel like your sense of self is being threatened. This happens to both parties involved in critical communication. Several factors may affect how you perceive your ego as stuck between a rock and a hard place.

"I must always be right." I once saw a set of couples' T-shirts. The men's T-shirt read "Mr. Right" and the women's T-shirt stated, "Mrs. Always Right". That may be a joke about the misconception that women feel they should always be right and despite it being entirely untrue, it does strike a chord. Your ego takes a knock when you slip up or are wrong about something. Yes, you are human, but nobody likes to admit being wrong. When confronting someone about accountability, they may feel their sense of self is at risk. They essentially have egg on their face and may feel embarrassed or as if they are somehow a bad person. They may feel ashamed and like being wrong is a fault instead of just a part of life. This "always right" attitude extends to leaders as well. Someone may point something out to you during a discussion; maybe you've made an assumption and jumped to a conclusion. Maybe it's that you don't have all your ducks in a row. Whatever the case, when you are approaching someone about their poor accountability, the last thing you want is to be told you're wrong about something.

"I have power." Arguing can be about a power struggle. You may find yourself arguing as an attempt to display your dominance. You want to assert yourself as being right and as being in a position of power over the other person. As a power display, you might want to have the final word, raise your voice to drown out the voices of others, or talk over them to show that what you have to say matters more. You might even use unreasonably harsh criticisms to crush their ego and make them back down as a result. Whether you are in a position of authority at work or you're tackling accountability with a friend, family member, or spouse; you must not allow a discussion to turn into a struggle for power. Using arguing as a display of power costs you the respect of others.

"You have to respect me." Respect is earned, not won in an argument. In fact, as I've just pointed out, arguing could lead to a loss of respect. When you argue, you are trying to make your voice heard, prove you are right, and protect your ego. You may think that making yourself heard and proving your point will garner respect from the person you are arguing down to, but the truth is it will likely only leave animosity brewing between you. As a leader, it is your responsibility to ensure you earn respect through being assertive, not by way of a verbal boxing match.

"I won't accept…" We all know the saying "Change what you can and accept what you can't." This idiom speaks volumes about the struggles we face with acceptance. We don't want to accept our faults, mistakes, or failures. We perceive them as a threat to our sense of self as if we are somehow of less value if we accept we've mucked up. The truth is that mistakes don't define our value as human beings. We all have the same intrinsic value. Despite putting people on pedestals and raising them to unrealistically high statuses, there is not a single person in this world who is worth more or less than any other person. When confronting someone or being confronted, it is important to reassure yourself or the other person that mistakes don't reduce their value as a person.

Stay on Point

Discussions can wander off into different directions and veer off point completely. It is vital to keep that crucial conversation train on track. The person you are talking to may want to bring points in which are not strictly relative to accountability. You may find yourself doing the same if you're the one being confronted. If you find the point drifting away and the conversation taking on a different direction, gently guide it back to what is being addressed. If you allow the conversation to branch off, the potency of your message becomes lost or you lose the message that is being conveyed to you. Ultimately, you end your meeting having achieved very little or nothing at all aside from confusing the matter.

Describe the Problem

I already told you how to define the problem in preparation for this critical discussion. Now it's time to describe the problem to the person you're dealing with according to that definition. It must be made explicitly clear what was expected of them and what happened or what didn't happen as a result of their actions. If you don't clearly set out what the problem is, you cannot expect someone to acknowledge there even is a problem or what part they had to play in the unfavorable results. In the same vein, if the other person doesn't have a clear understanding of the problem, they cannot effectively employ their problem-solving skills to come up with a way to fix it.

Find Points of Mutual Agreement

I didn't say reach an agreement. I said find points you both mutually agree on. Sometimes an agreement can be confused with finding a solution. What I mean is; find things in the discussion you can both agree on. These kinds of crucial conversations generally revolve around disagreements. Finding aspects of the situation you can mutually agree on shows that you are willing to keep an open mind. It can be something as simple as appreciating their point of view. That doesn't mean you have to agree that their point of view is the only correct one, it just means you show an understanding of where they are coming from. It may be that both of you want to see the business succeed and that every single person is a part of that success. Find positives to agree on instead of just focusing on the negatives, and if those positives can be motivation to find a solution, all the better.

Encourage Problem-Solving

Communication isn't a one-way street. It's not about you telling someone off for not being accountable, giving them the solution, and expecting results. Communication means engaging with someone and collaborating to find a mutually beneficial way to fix the problem. When you collaborate, you're not spoon-feeding the other person a solution. They don't learn anything from that experience. Why should they put their thinking cap on if you've already done all the mental heavy-lifting for them? What you would be doing is encouraging the other person to use their problem-solving skills to come up with solutions of their own. That doesn't mean you should leave it all up to them. You have to do your fair share and come up with solutions as well, but at least give them the chance to provide input on how to fix things. Prompt them to engage their brain by saying things like "How do you think we can solve this?" or"What do you think can be done about this?" or even"Where do we go from here?" You can use questions appropriate to the situation and make them more specific to the exact accountability problem at hand but it's important to involve the other person in the process.

Offer Assistance

Sometimes a solution is not as simple as deciding on what needs to change. There are times when people need assistance and coaching to make changes and stick to them. If you see that someone is going to need some help along the way to make progress in learning to take accountability, offer to help. Offering your assistance shows you understand they may face struggles and you are willing to help. It makes people feel valued and as if they aren't just being attacked and that, in turn, makes them more receptive to solutions.

Going Forward: Set SMART Goals

Whether you are working on your personal accountability or encouraging accountability in others, setting goals for making progress is vital for change and success. Setting goals may seem pretty straightforward at first, but if you don't know how to set them properly, you could be setting yourself and others up for failure. Most people think goal-setting is about deciding on their ultimate goal and simply working toward it. They couldn't be more wrong. Setting goals takes some mental legwork and a set of guidelines, but it's not tricky. I'm going to tell you how to do it and set yourself up for success.

You have to be SMART about setting goals. You can't just say you want to be more accountable and *poof*, it happens. You have to define your goals and create a blueprint to work by. Here's how to go about setting SMART goals.

What does SMART stand for?

- Specific.

- Measurable.

- Relevant.

- Time-bound.

Let's break it down into each individual component.

Specific

Have you ever set New Year's resolutions and failed to achieve them? Many people have trouble with this and by February they've thrown in the towel. The worst part is they don't understand why they're failing or what to do about it. Their self-esteem takes a knock and they just feel like they can't achieve anything they set out to achieve. The truth is they can, and you can too. The first thing you have to do is lose the habit of setting vague goals. Goals must be set out as clearly and in as much detail as possible.

Many people make losing weight or getting fit their New Year's resolution but that's all they define it as. It's vague and vague equates to useless. Why? Simple; if you don't know exactly where you're going, how are you ever going to get there? Instead of "lose weight," define how much weight you want to lose; "lose 15 pounds".

Instead of "get fit," be more specific, like "run a half marathon" or "bench press 100 pounds." The more specific you are about your goal, the easier it becomes to design a plan for getting there.

To help you create specific goals, ask yourself the following five W questions:

- What – What do you want to achieve?

- When – By when do you want to achieve the goal?

- Where – Where are you achieving your goal?

- Who – Who is involved in achieving this goal?

- Why – Why do you want to accomplish the goal?

In terms of accountability, break the problem down into the exact aspects you want to improve. Perhaps your ultimate goal is to stop pitching up to work late. If you don't define exactly what you need to stop or start doing to avoid arriving late, how are you going to squash your late-coming habit? In this particular case, you need to go more in-depth and create a detailed goal using the questions above. For example:

"I want to stop constantly pitching up late for work so that I maximize my productivity during work hours. That way I don't have to work outside of office hours, don't produce sub-standard work because I am always rushing to get things done in less time at the office, and don't miss out on meetings that result in me not knowing exactly what is going on in my team/company.

I can do this by creating a schedule for my time outside of work and sticking with it."

Can you see how you have been explicit in what you want to achieve, why you want to achieve it, and who is positively affected by successfully reaching your goal? Now you have a definite destination and you know what direction you have to go in to get there.

Measurable

Okay, you have a well-defined goal; you know exactly where you are heading and what you need to do to arrive at your destination. That's great! However, it's not nearly enough to make sure you actually get there. Your goal needs to be measurable. Different goals will have different means of measuring your progress. Setting a measurable goal ties in with being specific. If you aren't precise about your goal, you're not going to be able to know how close you are getting to achieving it.

To figure out how you're going to measure your progress, answer the following questions:

- How do you know if you've reached your goal?

- How much or how many?

- What indicates you're making progress?

Returning to the example above, how do you measure your progress in ditching the habit of arriving late for work?

You know you have reached your goal when you aren't arriving late for work unless under extreme or unavoidable circumstances. How many days you are arriving late indicates whether you are making progress or not.

Achievable

Many people make the mistake of setting goals they simply cannot reach at all or they can't do it in the time they give themselves to do it. Pitching up to work on time is an achievable goal but setting the goal of being a size two when you don't have a petite build is totally unattainable. Likewise, aiming for a 30-pound weight loss in two months is just not going to happen. You must be able to achieve the goal you set for yourself and to help you decide whether that goal is achievable, ask yourself the following questions:

Has anybody in a similar position ever successfully achieved this kind of goal before? It is important to put this question into the context of people with similar capabilities, resources, attributes, etc. to ensure you aren't setting a goal that is not achievable for you, personally. Just because someone completely different from yourself has achieved it before doesn't mean you are in a position to achieve it.

Do you have what it takes to reach your goal? If not, consider what you can do to make sure you get what it takes. – This question could refer to skills, physical capabilities, or resources for reaching a goal. Going back to late-coming, do you have the resources to get to work on time? For instance, if your car is unreliable, you may not have the resources but you can have it fixed so that you do.

Relevant

All goals must be relevant to you. Workplace accountability is relevant because you want to keep your job so that you can keep a roof over your head, food on the table, and gas in the tank. You might want to improve your workplace relationships with your colleagues and boss to make your working environment more pleasant. Another reason you may want to become more accountable at work is to set yourself up for climbing the career ladder and make yourself a candidate for promotion. On a more personal note, you may want to become more accountable to preserve and improve relationships with friends and family.

Making the goal relevant to you means you're motivated to achieve it. If you don't care about the goal, why would you want to put in the time and effort to successfully reach it?

Time-Bound

This is another biggie that many people overlook when setting goals. They neglect to set a time limit for achieving their goal. If you know what you want to achieve, can measure it, and it is attainable, but you don't set a timeframe to do it in, what motivation do you have to really put the effort in to reach that goal efficiently? Without a time limit, you could spend the next two years trying to stop pitching up late for work all the time. Yes, you want to stop the habit, but you aren't under any pressure to achieve it and there's an attitude of "I'm working on it. I have made some progress. I'll eventually get there."

Some goals will have a deadline that may not be within your control to decide. Your boss/team may give you a deadline by which they expect you to be arriving on time for work every day. You will be able to set your own deadline for more personal accountability goals. The important thing is to set a definite time limit.

Write a Personal Mission Statement

You can use mission statements for achieving personal goals or ask the person you are confronting about accountability to do. It doesn't have to be something they hand in as a contract with you or the company. It's more of a personal contract with themselves or if you are writing one for personal goals, yourself.

Why is a mission statement an effective and helpful tool for reaching your goals? It helps you set out exactly what you want to achieve and why. Use your SMART goals to develop your mission statement. Keep in mind that a mission statement isn't a blueprint for achieving your goals. You're not going for a lengthy statement about how you're going to go about doing it, you're just writing out a kind of personal contract with yourself. The act of putting pen to paper and actually writing out your mission statement, in itself, tends to make you more serious about reaching your goal. There is just something about writing down your intentions that solidifies your resolve to commit to achieving success and amps up your motivation to be successful in your venture.

Here's what a mission statement for the above example of late-coming would look like:

"In the next two months, I am going to reduce the number of days I pitch up late for work until I arrive on time every day. I have the ability and resources to make this happen. I want to achieve this goal because arriving late hurts my career success as well as the performance of my team. I also want to position myself favorably for promotion so that I can advance my career within the company."

A mission statement doesn't have to be a lengthy affair. Having too much waffle in your statement dilutes your goal and can encourage you to veer off track. It's not a journal entry, it's a concise summary of what you want to achieve.

Tip: Write your mission statement down by hand instead of typing it up on a computer. You use a lot more sensory information and concentration when you write something down by hand. This helps it stick in your memory and makes it more personal to boost your commitment to achieving your goal. Believe it or not, writing your goal down encourages you to hold yourself accountable for reaching that goal. In the case of accountability, it's already a small step toward improving your accountability!

Create a Blueprint for Success

You know what has to be done and why you want to do it. You've made sure you have what you need to get it done and you've set out a timeline. You also know how to measure the progress you're making toward achieving your goal. Now it's time to create a blueprint of how you're going to reach that goal. It's time to brainstorm and fire up those problem-solving skills.

When you're dealing with holding someone else accountable, allow them to offer their own solutions for the problem. Putting your heads together to figure out how they can improve their accountability creates opportunities for coming up with more possible fixes than you or they may be able to think of alone. Helping find solutions also shows you're interested and willing to help them make a success of their accountability goals instead of throwing them into the deep end by saying "This is the problem, fix it."

Let's go back to that habit of arriving late for work all the time. Your blueprint may involve:

- Saving up to have your car fixed.

- Budgeting for regular maintenance once it is running up to snuff.

- Getting up and leaving for work earlier in the morning to account for or beat rush hour traffic.

- Finding a different route to take to bypass heavily congested travel routes.

- Packing all your paraphernalia the night before to save time in the morning. For example, pre-packing your lunch, setting out your clothes for the next day, and making sure critical items such as car keys or public transport tickets are in a place that is easy to find.

These are just a few examples of possible lifestyle or habit changes that may help improve accountability in this particular situation. You need to really explore all your options relevant to the specific problem you are addressing in order to set your own SMART goals.

Chapter 5:

Creating Accountability in Others

Now that you know how to approach someone about their lack of accountability, you need to learn how to build accountability in others. Building a culture of accountability around you, whether in your personal or professional life, is vital to personal and organizational success. As I've demonstrated to you, no interpersonal relationship and no business can succeed when accountability is nonexistent. So, how do you go about building that culture of accountability and encouraging others to be accountable?

Lead by Example

The idea of leading by example is often seen as an authoritarian role. The people in leadership positions, those who are respected, higher-ups, and even people we place on pedestals like celebrities are often expected to be the ones to lead by example. However, you can lead by example in any relationship. You may not be the boss in your team but you can show others the way by being accountable yourself. You may be an equal in your relationships with family and friends, but you can still set the example of what you expect in the relationship.

If you are in a leadership position, however, leading by example becomes your responsibility. It actually becomes a form of accountability. You are holding yourself accountable for the influence you have on those working under your authority. Let's revisit that all-important question from the first chapter.

"How can I hold anyone else accountable if I don't hold myself accountable?"

Leading by example isn't going to create a culture of accountability by itself. It is, however, the first crucial step you must take toward building accountability in others. If you can walk the walk and talk the talk, you will earn respect, trust, and the right to check others on their accountability issues instead of fostering the attitude of "If you don't do it, why should I?"

Leadership Accountability: The 5 C's

The lack of accountability has spread through modern society and culture like a disease. It addles our social structure and relationships, weakening every aspect of our lives. It's pretty much become a social norm to be late, break promises, miss deadlines, be forgetful, shirk responsibility, and not follow through. It's a problem that can be found in both the professional and personal spheres of our lives. The following section is about the five C's of leadership accountability, but these principles can be applied to your personal relationships just as effectively. So, without further ado, let's dive in.

Common Purpose

The first thing you need to do to encourage accountability in others is to give them something to buy into. This comes down to the WIIFM principle. If there is any single universal question every person asks about anything they do, it's "What's in it for me?" You may think it's a no-brainer in an organizational context. You do your job, you get paid. You do your job well, you stand a chance of advancing your career. It seems a simple enough concept to grasp, but what you have to understand is that people can lose sight of why they're doing what they're doing and why they should be accountable.

As a leader, it's easy to forget to encourage your team to buy into doing something and doing it well. After all, you're the boss, they have to do what you tell them to, right? To a certain extent, yes, but that doesn't mean they have to be passionate about it. Knowing what you have to do because you're told to do it doesn't inspire a good work ethic, quality performance, or accountability.

What you need to do is explain to your team why it's important. Each and every employee has a role to play in organizational success. Tell them why they matter to the company. Give them a reason to not only do the work but to do it to the best of their ability or even go above and beyond just what is expected of them. Giving individual team members the "why" they're important provides them with a sense that they're not just another brick in the wall and makes them feel like they belong, because they matter. Explaining to your team the reason they matter; explaining their "why," creates a common purpose for every individual to work toward.

Clear Expectations

I've mentioned it before and I'll do it again; you cannot hold anybody accountable if your expectations aren't made crystal clear. It opens the door for excuses if someone doesn't have all the details of exactly what they're expected to do. You aren't giving them a solid framework for holding themselves accountable and you're giving them the option not to. Setting clear expectations requires good communication between you and your team as well as between individual team members. You can expect to have to reiterate these expectations more than once. That doesn't mean your team is thick. It just means that everybody is working toward proper communication that leaves no room for misunderstandings. So how do you set out clear expectations for your staff?

Clarify what you expect, down to the very last little detail. Don't leave any aspect of your expectations open to personal interpretation. Remember, individual interpretation doesn't necessarily point to a lack of accountability. If someone is convinced that you want something done one way, they're going to do it that way. They may not realize they are not doing what you actually want them to do. This is different from being confused or knowing they don't have all the information and blundering on anyway and then using the excuse of "I didn't know." When someone interprets what you say in a certain way and later it comes out that interpretation was wrong; some of the onus is on you to take accountability for not being clear enough in expressing your expectations.

Define what success should look like when your staff does what they are expected to do. You may have told them exactly what they need to do but you haven't provided them with a measure of the quality of work you expect of them. They could easily produce mediocre work while still doing what you expect them to do.

Communication

In *Crucial Communication*, I explain the importance of good communication and I teach you how to communicate effectively. Accountability and success require constant good communication between a leader and their team. You can't just bring your team together to work toward a common purpose, set out clear expectations, and then leave them to their own devices. It doesn't work that way.

People lose focus, they may lose sight of the end goal, and their motivation may even wane. It's your job, as a leader, to constantly communicate with your team. That doesn't mean you have to helicopter or micromanage, which I'll get into a bit later in this chapter. What it does mean is that you need to keep them on the right track, ask for feedback on their progress and any obstacles they're facing, and remind them of that all-important "why." Remind them that they matter as individuals and that what the entire team is working towards matters.

Collaboration and Coaching

Part of being a good leader is not just trying to make your team do what you tell them to do but being able to work with them to achieve that common purpose I mentioned above. An aspect of collaborating is offering to coach. Keep track of what your team is doing and the progress they are making. Encourage them to bring any obstacles to your attention. Nobody is perfect and that's why you need to work together to achieve success. Don't think of coaching as a professor giving a lecture at a university. What I mean here is listening more than you're talking. Talk only about 20% of the time and actively listen for the other 80%. You will only be able to truly pick up on what is really going on if you listen and observe.

As a leader, you need to support your team and not just expect them to go it alone once they've been given instructions. Part of holding yourself accountable is being responsible for giving your team the support they need to uphold their own accountability.

Consequences

Consequences can be positive. The word has earned itself a bad reputation because it's generally used to indicate negative outcomes but that's all it is. Consequence is simply another word for outcomes, the result of what you do or don't do. I've just explained that you need to communicate with your staff and tell them what success will look like. This is where consequences come in. They need to know what is going right and not just what is going wrong. Highlight wins, no matter how small. Celebrate them so your team isn't just brought under fire when something flops. Focusing on the negative creates a negative attitude and lackluster performance. Why should they want to do well when it's just glossed over and not acknowledged?

If something is going wrong, communicate, collaborate, coach. Ask your team for their input and how everyone can work together to get things back on track for success. Don't just bark orders and tell them how things will be done to correct the problem. You run a team and that makes you a part of that team. Allow everybody to contribute ideas and solutions, not just yourself.

Build Trust

I've already explained that accountability is a source of trust. Trust is also part of accountability. You need to be accountable to earn the trust of others. At the same time, you need to extend trust to others and allow them to be accountable for their actions.

When you look at needs, there are both organizational needs and employee needs within a company. Both sets of needs are equally important. Trust is one of the important organizational needs that must be met for your business to run as a well-oiled machine.

Organizational needs:

- Clarity.

- Culture.

- Purpose.

- Recognition.

- Trust.

Employee needs:

- A sense of belonging.

- A sense of contribution.

- Feeling enabled or empowered.

- Feeling that you matter.

- Feel respected.

Trust is important in any organization, not only for accountability but also for:

- Effective teamwork.

- Employee retention (lower your employee turnover which creates discord in the workplace).

- Individual employee, team, and organizational resilience.

- Productivity.

Now that we understand the role of trust in the workplace, let's get into what you can do to build trust with your team. Bear in mind that all of these ways of building trust are rooted in accountability. You must hold yourself accountable for taking these steps, not only to build trust but to prove you are a person who is dependable and takes ownership of your actions.

Steps for Building Trust

Be honest: Honesty means being straightforward with your staff, not beating about the bush, and not omitting anything. Sugar-coating mistakes and poor behavior or results provide a false sense of security and when the hammer inevitably comes down on the employee or team, they're going to feel betrayed even if you didn't technically lie. Beating about the bush leaves people feeling confused. Omitting details about anything makes others feel they won't get the whole story from you and will always wonder if there's anything you're not telling them. Being caught in an outright lie is the easiest way to destroy your credibility and kill all trust your team has in you.

Don't play *Gossip Girl*: The television series *Gossip Girl* is based on the lives of teenagers plagued by an anonymous online figure calling themself Gossip Girl. All the juicy, scandalous details of the goings-on in the lives of these teens are sent in as tips and published for the world to see and know about. Your life and workplace may not be a teen drama, but the principle stays the same. Gossiping behind others' backs turns those you work with against you. This is especially damaging when you're in a leadership position. Your staff will feel they cannot openly communicate with you or come to you when they are facing problems, both at work or at home, which will impact their performance.

Do what you say you'll do or as you're expected to do: Not following through with what you say you're going to do can sometimes be taken as a lie. Wouldn't you feel lied to if someone intentionally says they will do something, knowing full-well what they're letting themselves in for, but don't follow through? Your team will feel the same way and your credibility and reliability will go down the drain as well. Similarly, if you are fully aware of what is expected of you but you just don't do it, others will feel slighted and not trust you to step up to the plate and meet expectations.

Own up to mistakes and uncertainties: We're all human. We all make mistakes. Yes, even you. Leaders aren't infallible or perfect. It's better to show your human side and own up to your mistakes. Trust me when I say your employees don't think you're perfect. Admitting fault will earn you their respect and trust. Likewise, leaders aren't omnipotent. Nobody knows everything. Being accountable means admitting you're not all-knowing and are also prepared to grow and learn. Pretending you know something when you really don't is the same thing as lying in some people's eyes. Remember that the next time you're tempted to fib about your knowledge to save face.

Trust others: In the previous section, I mentioned keeping track of the progress your team is making toward the goals you've set. There is a huge difference between keeping your finger on the pulse of what's going on and being a helicopter boss or micromanager. Nobody likes a boss who is forever hovering over and breathing down their necks. Not only is it uncomfortable but it can also create tension and animosity. The same thing happens if you try to micromanage everything. Not only are you putting too much pressure on yourself; you are annoying your staff and annoyance breeds disgruntled feelings.

When you don't allow your staff members to work autonomously and make decisions, you are showing them that you don't trust them to get the job done or produce quality work on their own. When I say working autonomously and making decisions, it's within reason, of course. You can't allow someone to make decisions that are out of their scope of power. What you can do is define their scope of decision-making and then let them make decisions within that range. In doing so, you are empowering your team and showing them that you trust them. Trust is a two-way street. You need to trust your staff and they need to trust you.

Trust yourself: How can you expect anybody else to put their faith in you when you don't even trust yourself? Trusting yourself comes from a place of assertiveness and confidence. You must be confident that you can do your job and be secure in the decisions you make. When you start wavering about whether you can or can't, or whether you are making the right decisions, your team will not be able to trust you to lead them effectively. When your leadership is second-guessed, your influence and credibility suffer.

Trust Building Exercises

While trust is earned by being accountable and doing, or not doing, everything we've just discussed, there are fun exercises you can do with your team to improve and bolster trust in the workplace. Try some of the following exercises as a fun way to get your team working together and trusting each other. Remember, trust isn't built overnight, especially if there are existing trust issues within the team, but using team-building exercises is a fun way to start repairing that trust.

Important note: Building trust in your team means you take part in them as well. You're one member of the team and you need to show that to them. You need to show your team that you trust them as much as you expect them to trust each other and that they can also trust you. So go ahead, try these exercises, and be part of the fun!

Minefield

This trust-building exercise is ideal for smaller teams.

- Divide everyone up into pairs.

- Lay out an obstacle course or "minefield" using non-breakable objects such as chairs, cones, or even paper cups.

- One member of each pair stands at the opposite end of the minefield and is blindfolded.

- The other person in the pair guides their blindfolded mate around the obstacles by calling out directions and movements to get them safely to the other side.

- Once the first person completes the course, they swap around and do it again so that everybody gets a turn to be blindfolded and trust someone else's guidance.

Willow in the Wind

This activity is ideal for medium-sized groups of at least eight participants.

- Pick someone to be the "willow" and stand them in the center of a circle created by the other team members.

- Blindfold the willow and have them cross their arms across their chest.

- Have the other people extend their arms out in front of them, ready to prop up the willow.

- When both the willow and the supporters are ready, the willow begins to fall, trusting their peers to keep them from falling by gently pushing them upright again.

The willow should be allowed to fall in various directions so everybody gets a chance to help support them. It doesn't have to be just one person who pushes the willow back upright, it can be two or even three at a time. The idea is to build trust by not allowing the willow to fall.

Human Pinball

This exercise is best suited for larger groups of at least 10 or more participants.

- Get everyone to stand in a circle, not too close together but not too far apart either.

- Pick one person to be the "human pinball." Blindfold them and have them cross their arms over their chest.

- Start with the human pinball on one side of the circle.

- The person closest to them gently pushes them in a direction and they must walk in that direction.

- Inevitably the human pinball will reach the other side of the circle and the next person turns them around and sends them off in another direction with a gentle push.

Two Truths, One Lie

- Have everybody take turns telling the group three statements about themselves. Two of the statements should be true and one should be a lie.

- Everybody else takes turns guessing which statement of the three is the lie.

- To keep the fun going and to give everybody a chance to have a guess, don't reveal the lie until everybody has weighed in on the statements.

- Try to limit each person's guess to around five seconds to prevent the activity from dragging on indefinitely.

Setting up for Accountability Success

Accountability isn't just about confronting an issue when one crops up. Old sayings stick around because of how true they are and this one has been around since the early 17th century; "Prevention is better than cure." Okay, history lesson over. The point I'm making is that you need to set yourself and your team up for success when you're trying to create a culture of accountability in the workplace instead of just putting fires out. Once you create that accountability culture, there will be way fewer fires that need putting out. So, how do you create that culture of accountability and what does it look like?

This Is What Accountability Culture Looks Like

There are 10 signs you have a culture of accountability in your organization.

1. Each individual clearly understands the role they play in the team and what the expectations are.

2. Each person has the information and the means to do their job and they feel confident about asking for anything they need.

3. The whole team agrees on their common purpose by collectively weighing in on goals and priorities.

4. Everybody clearly understands the organization's core values and those values are reflected in the way they perform.

5. Nobody is ever surprised by the team's results because everyone can see the progress being made at all times.

6. Progress and results are reviewed together in regular team meetings where everybody has a voice.

7. Ongoing improvement and opportunities for personal growth and development are regularly discussed.

8. There is trust between team members and team leaders to produce the expected results and individuals feel confident to ask for help if they need it.

9. Every member of the team, including the team leader, openly welcomes and freely shares feedback.

10. Different teams working toward the same common purpose work together effectively to achieve results.

Building a Culture of Accountability

Now that you know what a culture of accountability looks like, it's time to get to work building one in your team and organization.

Pick the Right Person

This has to be your first port of call. Picking the right person for the job is crucial to achieving success and being able to hold that person accountable for the results. This means knowing each employee and understanding their strengths, weaknesses, and skills. It's pointless getting someone who has the charisma of a rock to try to deal with disgruntled clients or present a new marketing strategy. You are setting an employee up for failure if you assign them a task that you know isn't within their scope of strengths.

Now, that's not to say you shouldn't challenge your team and individual staff members. The only way for someone to grow is to be challenged and learn how to overcome those challenges. Part of leading is stepping into the role of mentor. However, knowing your employees well will give you a better understanding of what they can handle as a challenge and what they are sure to fail at. As a leader, it is your responsibility to navigate that fine line between challenging someone, knowing they have the ability to succeed, and pushing them to do something you have a pretty good idea they can't do.

Equally important is knowing who can perform best in certain situations. You may have several team members who are capable but one may stand out as the best candidate for the job. It's crucial to give the task to the person who can do it best when it comes to taking care of important tasks where you can't risk anything going wrong.

Get Commitment

Once you have picked the right person for the job, you need to get their full commitment. Getting someone's full commitment requires you to:

- Understand what makes the employee want to give you their full commitment.

- Clearly set out your expectations.

- Define what success looks like.

- Get them to buy into the task by understanding how it benefits them by benefitting the team and organization.

- Motivate them to commit 100% by understanding their value and get them excited about taking on the task.

Why is getting commitment so important for accountability? When you buy into something and are fully committed to it, you are motivated to take accountability for your actions. When getting someone to commit, don't accept a wishy-washy "I'll try." That answer tells you they aren't fully committed or motivated. Don't ask "Are you going to do…" because that leaves room for that noncommittal "I'll try." Be direct. Ask the person, "Do I have your full 100% commitment to…"

Praise and Consequences

You will never create a culture of accountability without praise for quality performance and consequences for regular poor performance. Many people are motivated by positive praise and reward for good performance. They may also be motivated by a desire to avoid negative consequences. Just like you need to create clear expectations, you need to create clear reinforcement and consequences. Not only that, those consequences are pretty useless if you don't follow through with them. Your staff will quickly catch on to the empty threats and not take accountability seriously. Being a leader can be a tough job. It's up to you to have those uncomfortable discussions and ultimately dole out consequences to prove you mean business.

Let's talk about praise. You aren't going to create motivation and a happy workforce without praise. It can be easy to overlook good performance when it's expected, but that's not going to make your employees happy campers. Yes, they get paid to do their job, but that doesn't mean they have to do more than the minimum and produce mediocre quality work. You need to light a fire under them and get them to go that extra mile by using praise and reward.

Tell someone they've done a good job to show them you notice the effort they put in and that you value their contribution. Not all companies implement a rewards system but it's not a bad idea. Rewards can range from acknowledgement as the employee of the month, a cash bonus for producing the best work out of the team, or even extra time off. The trick is to find out what motivates each employee. What do they want that will make them go the extra mile? For some, a simple pat on the back is enough to make them feel good. Maybe a parent would appreciate some extra time off to spend with their children. Maybe someone is saving up for something and really wants a cash bonus. Personalized rewards for stand-out performance are the best way to promote the same level of enthusiasm and drive in every member of your team. After all, if they don't care about the reward, why would they strive for it?

Feedback

Giving and receiving feedback cannot be stressed enough when you're trying to create a culture of accountability. You need to be able to take feedback and create a safe environment where employees feel they can come to you with their feedback, even if what they have to say isn't all sunshine and roses. You need to be able to take feedback on your personal performance as a leader as well as about the working environment, expectations, or anything really, whether it's good or bad. Getting feedback from staff is also an opportunity to get a different perspective on things. They are your eyes and ears on the ground, so to speak. You may also receive some valuable ideas and solutions to problems from them. Just because you're in charge doesn't mean you shouldn't listen to the people working under your management. Those people are the source of your organizational success.

Now, getting feedback is only half the equation. You need to be able to give constructive feedback as well. Constructive feedback doesn't just mean addressing a problem when it arises. It means talking to employees about their good performance, the areas you think they are excelling in, and what you think their strengths are. Providing consistent feedback is the perfect way to keep everybody on track and dealing with challenges before molehills turn into mountains.

Equal Accountability

One thing that creates a divide in teams is a sense of inequality or victimization and favoritism. Everybody must be held equally accountable. You cannot constantly come down on some employees while you allow others off the hook. Your credibility as a leader will take a knock and you are guaranteed to lose the respect of those you're constantly holding accountable as they watch you let it slide for others. Inequality fosters animosity between coworkers which makes your team dysfunctional.

Some instances of accountability inequality may include:

- Being harsher on newcomers than on employees who have been with the company so long they're "part of the furniture."

- Being stricter with lower-ranking employees than with higher-ups.

- Bringing the hammer down on less skilled employees while letting highly skilled accountability offenders off the hook.

Favoring those with more experience or skills, those who are more social, or those who are in more senior positions shows other employees that you value them more.

A Framework for Accountability

Before I can tell you how to develop an accountability framework, I need to explain what it is. It's a framework that designates who has ownership over which responsibilities and is in charge of reporting progress on those responsibilities being carried out. The role of an accountability framework is:

- To define the common purpose the team is working toward.

- Explaining the reason for the outcomes of that common purpose.

- Identifying how the information will be gathered and the progress monitored.

- To inform staff whether an evaluation of the progress and results is planned or not.

Accountability frameworks are ideally suited for projects a team is working on but how do they work? These frameworks assist with:

- Providing clear explanations of methods of gathering information and the expected timelines so that projects are implemented, overseen, managed, and reviewed.

- Encouraging decision-making and management of the project based on evidence and outcomes.

- Determining whether the project is performing and getting the desired results.

- Creating a platform for assessing how the project is progressing from an objective perspective.

Now that you know what it is and how it works, let's dig into how you create your accountability framework for your team's next project or goal. This kind of accountability framework is best suited for teams who work on projects for clients but with a little creativity, you can adapt it to other situations. When adapting this accountability framework, you could leave out parts of the framework that don't really apply to the purpose you're creating it for. To help develop a framework specific to your purpose, get your team involved in brainstorming how to best structure it to suit your needs.

1. **Establish the purpose of the project/goal.**

Part	Included Information
Purpose	This part of the framework sets out the who, what, and why.
	Why are you undertaking this project or setting this goal?
	What is the project or goal meant to achieve or what outcomes are you aiming for?
	Who are the project's clients? (This question is only applicable if your project has clients.)

In this first section of the framework, you want to establish:

- What need(s) the project or goal addresses.

- What the project or goal should achieve and how those outcomes will be achieved.

- Who the project or goal is aimed at.

2. Establish who the project/goal is aimed at and who will be involved.

Part	Included Information
Clients Beneficiaries Primary stakeholders	Clients and beneficiaries: What are the characteristics of the clients you are working for or those who will benefit from the outcomes.
	Primary stakeholders: Decide what external parties or departments within the organization are interested in the clients or beneficiaries, the project or goal, and why they are interested.

This section is aimed at projects of goals that fall into two categories; people and economic or business development.

If the project is aimed at people, try identifying all possible useful information that will give you a detailed picture of the target audience:

- Who they are.

- How large the target audience is.

- Gender.

- Age.

- Social position/characteristics.

- Economic position/characteristics.

- Geographical placement.

- Demographics.

If the project is aimed at business or economic development, try to identify the targeted areas or audiences as clearly as possible:

- What is the type of business you're developing?

- What are the characteristics of the business?

- What sector of the economy is the business in?

- The geographical location of the business.

- Clients or beneficiaries of the business.

- Demographics of the business's services or products as per the above criteria.

When it comes to the primary stakeholder section of this part of the framework, identify information like:

- Who your partner(s) are in executing the project or reaching the goal.

- Organizations or departments that already offer similar services or services that compliment what the project aims to provide.

- Lobbyists in favor of the targeted businesses the project is meant to develop.

- How the interested organization, department, or group is involved with the business development.

3. Determine responsibilities and accountabilities.

Part	Included Information
Accountabilities	The responsibilities and roles of those involved in completing the project or reaching the goal.
	How collaborative relationships with other partners, departments, or organizations involved will be managed.
	Methods of decision-making.
	Processes to make sure other partners perform as expected.

Under the accountabilities part of the framework, you need to identify:

- The team/organization/department responsible for carrying out the project.

- The team/organization/department that is accountable for the results being achieved even if they are not involved in carrying out the procedures that get those results.

- The decisions involved in carrying out the project.

- When parties collaborate on a project, determine who gets to have the final say in decision-making.

- Collaborating parties must decide whether or not the authority is going to be delegated and if so what the criteria for delegation is.

4. Develop a logic model.

Part	Included Information
Logic model	A logic model is an easy-to-read and accessible visual representation of: • The resources you have available to you. • What is going to be done with those resources. • The products of what is done with the resources. • The desired results of those actions.

Here's a table to give you a basic idea of what a logic model would look like for a project aimed at employee skill development:

Resources	Skilled and experienced internal or external coaches/trainers.
Processes	Providing training sessions for employees.
Direct products of the processes	The number of employees that have been trained and equipped with the desired skills.
Short-term results	Increased team or departmental productivity/efficacy/work quality.
Mid-term results	Increased organizational productivity/revenue generation.
Long-term results	Expanding the organization according to growth target.

This is a very basic example of a logic model but you get the idea.

5. Measure progress against targets.

Part	Included Information		
Measurements and targets	The means of measuring the quantity or quality of the direct products of the processes as outlined in the logic model to assess progress toward the target set for those process products.	Measurement:

Quantity: The number of trained employees.

Quality: The level of skills acquired by the trained employees. | Target:

The number of trained employees the company wants.

The level of skill the company wants employees to have. |
| | The means of measuring the quantity or quality of the | Measurement:

Short- | Target:

How |

Part	Included Information		
	short-, mid-, and long-term results outlined in the logic model to assess progress toward the targets set for each.	term: How much the productivity and efficacy of a team/department have increased or how much the quality of work has increased.	much work the team/department aims to get done in a set amount of time or the quality of work they are aiming for.
		Mid-term: How much the organization's productivity has increased or how much more revenue it's	How productive the team/department wants to be or how

Part	Included Information		
		generating. Long-term: How much the company has expanded or how close it is to expanding.	much money it wants to generate in a set amount of time. How much the company wants to grow within a set amount of time.

Targets should be set using the SMART goals principle I covered in Chapter 4. That is the only way you will be able to set proper goals and figure out how to measure your progress toward them.

6. Monitor performance.

Part	Included Information

Part	Included Information
Monitoring performance	Draw up a detailed plan of what information will be collected and used to monitor performance, how that information will be used to measure progress, and how often progress will be monitored.

When drawing up a plan for monitoring performance, be sure to include who will be collecting this information and drawing up performance reports and who will get these reports to use them.

7. Evaluate performance.

Part	Included Information
Evaluation	Decide whether performance will be evaluated or not. Give staff explanations of why or why not. If performance will be evaluated, determine when it will be evaluated.

You may or may not need to evaluate the performance of a project, but you should always consider evaluation. Sure, performance monitoring tells you whether you are making progress or not. However, evaluating performance can also help answer the question of why performance isn't up to scratch or if things could be done better or more efficiently, even if targets are being met.

Employee Performance Metrics

Employee performance metrics refer to how you measure an employee's performance in the workplace. Different industries will have different metrics specific to their niche but there are a few metrics you can use across the board no matter what your organization does.

Efficiency: To measure an employee's efficiency, you need to look at aspects such as time management, meeting deadlines, and their ability to prioritize and even delegate if that is within their power. Is time managed appropriately and deadlines met on time? Is the employee excelling at time management and bringing things in ahead of deadlines? Are you noticing that deadlines are pushed for extensions or missed because time isn't managed properly and tasks aren't prioritized?

Effectiveness: How effective is your employee? To help you determine the level of an employee's effectiveness, look at indicators like attendance and problem-solving. Can this person meet challenges head-on and find ways to overcome obstacles to get the work done or do they get stuck and battle to find their way around it?

Goal-based objectives: Are you working with your employee to set goals that align with the organization's goals and are they reaching those goals?

Work quality: When an employee delivers poor work quality, it affects the whole team and the organization.

Is this person meeting the work quality standards they are expected to?

Feedback: Is your employee actively asking you for feedback on their performance or are they not interested in what anybody else has to say?

Learning and growth: Along with actively asking for feedback, does this person want to learn and grow to improve their performance and advance their career, or are they just coasting along at the same speed they've always done? If an employee has been for training, are they putting the new knowledge and skills into action or just doing the same old thing they've always done?

Initiative: Does your employee take initiative within their scope of authority? Do they step up to the plate and do things of their own initiative or are they always waiting to be told to do it? Do they go the extra mile or only put in the minimum that is expected of them? Are they bringing new, fresh ideas to the table?

Consistency: Does your employee consistently perform to the same standard or is their performance all over the place like a ping-pong ball?

Overtime: Not working overtime shouldn't be used as an indicator of poor performance. After all, your employee could be excelling in every other aspect. However, it could be taken as a bonus feather in their performance cap if you do notice they are putting in the extra hours to make sure things get done.

Teamwork: Let's face it, it can be a dog-eat-dog world out there and a case of every person for themselves. Climbing the ladder is about looking after number one, but number one isn't all that matters. Does this person "play well with others" and offer help freely to achieve team and organizational goals?

Communication: An organization cannot run without communication. Does your employee communicate well and effectively or do they clam up and sit in the corner without offering input, sharing information, or asking for what they need to get the work done?

Accountability roadblocks

We often face roadblocks when holding ourselves accountable and holding others accountable. Why do we struggle with accountability? What is standing in our way? Clarity is one of the biggest accountability stumbling blocks and here's why:

- **Time:** It takes time to clarify and be clear. Whether you're giving someone a task or accepting a task, nailing down the specifics takes time and we often don't want to spend time hashing out all the little details.

- **Effort:** This one is a big loophole for personal accountability. If someone asks you to do something that may require more effort than you really want to put in, being vague about what you're going to do and when you're going to do it gives you a way out. After all, if you haven't committed to specifics, how can anybody hold you accountable?

- **Feelings:** As a leader, pushing someone to make a clear commitment to the task you are giving them may seem like you're being pushy or aggressive. You want to "be nice" and you let them walk away without being clear on what they are committing to or that they have fully committed.

- **Comparison:** The grass may seem greener on the other side. Giving someone clear specifics of what is expected of them may mean they do only what is expected. If you leave a little wiggle room, you might be pleasantly surprised if they go above and beyond.

Chapter 6:

Virtual Accountability

The world has become increasingly virtual. It started with social media and messaging apps and crept into every aspect of our lives, including the workplace. In this modern virtual era, accountability has become more important than ever. When you're working with remote employees, it's a totally different ball game from working in a brick and mortar office space. Let's take a look at how virtual workspaces affect employees and accountability to help you keep your online team on track.

Challenges Virtual Teams Face

Understanding the challenges you and your team face is the first step to overcoming them. I'm going to tell you what these challenges often are and offer tips for tackling them.

First of all, let's take stock of the many types of virtual communication:

- Email.

- Instant message apps.

- Online project management software.

- Social media.

- Video conferencing.

- Voice calls.

Communication is a vital component of accountability. With so many ways to communicate virtually with your employees, why is it so challenging to promote a culture of accountability in your team? Several contributing factors can make virtual accountability challenging.

Too many types of communication are used: Using too many forms of communication makes it difficult to find and reference information being passed around. How can you hold employees accountable when they're regularly confused about where information is and what method to use to get in touch with you or their colleagues? The problem is further compounded by the fact that text-based virtual communication doesn't allow the interpretation of body language or tone, and poor communication skills may lead to lengthy messages in which the point gets lost.

Distractions: Yes, employees are responsible for managing distractions at home but that doesn't mean they'll be perfect at it. Interruptions from family members, deliveries, pets, etc. can easily derail time management for even the most diligent employee.

Isolation: Workplace relationships are a core part of creating a cohesive team that can hold each other accountable. Feeling lonely and isolated can make employees feel despondent and unhappy which, in turn, affects their productivity and performance. Happy workers are more likely to be accountable.

Company culture suffers: That friendly company culture, friendships with coworkers, and real-time interaction in the flesh create a positive company culture. All of this either diminishes or completely dies when you're working remotely. Staff morale and motivation go with it which affects performance, employee contentedness, and staff's ability/willingness to hold each other accountable.

Technological difficulties: We all know how frustrating technology can be even though we rely on it for almost everything. When your technology goes belly-up, your ability to work and communicate goes with it. Your performance dips and accountability becomes harder.

Time zones: Many online companies employ staff from all corners of the globe. You can't honestly expect employees to change their working hours to fit a single timezone, especially when they have families. Doing that means they're working when their friends and family are asleep and they're asleep when their family is spending time together without them. This adds to feeling isolated and performance nosedives. It also takes longer to communicate with one another if you're waiting for an employee or colleague to wake up and start their day while it's afternoon already on your side of the world. Real-time communication becomes pretty much impossible.

Tips for Overcoming Virtual Workplace Challenges

Maintaining a culture of accountability in a virtual world can be challenging, but it isn't impossible. Here's how to promote accountability in a remote team:

Categorize Types of Communication

Using too many different types of communication for all sorts of work-related purposes quickly becomes confusing. Consider each type of virtual communication and what it's best suited for. Define what types of communication are used for what kinds of information to make it easier to reference information when needed. For example, you can use video conferencing for team meetings and progress check-ups while you can use instant messaging for quick questions. Project management tools or email might be best used for communicating about a specific task.

Manage Them As People

As a leader, it's important to maintain communication and an active relationship with every member of your team. I mentioned cultivating individual relationships with staff members to build trust. That doesn't change when your workspace goes virtual. Trust, open communication, and feeling like a valued member of a team or organization can improve accountability, so don't just manage your employees like a message on a screen. Manage them like the real people they are.

Encourage Virtual Sociability

Sure, some introverts won't really socialize with colleagues in the office, and working remotely makes it even easier to avoid being social. However, for the most part, encouraging social interaction online will help diminish feelings of isolation and loneliness. It also helps build team cohesion because coworkers can maintain friendships and feel more connected. It can be something as simple as a work or team chat group where staff can chit-chat and even share music, images, and other feel-good information or media.

Keep Things Transparent

There are a variety of virtual project management platforms available to online businesses today. Picking an appropriate platform or software to keep everybody in the loop is a must, but keeping things transparent is crucial for team accountability. Part of accountability comes from team members holding each other accountable. Pick a software that allows everybody to see what everybody else is doing, within reason. When they can't see what others are doing and nobody can see what they're doing, how are they going to hold each other accountable?

Make Information Accessible

Everybody should be able to access all information related to a specific project or general work. Everybody is in the know and you keep up that transparency I just mentioned. There are several information-sharing tools available, such as Google Drive. Pick a tool that suits your needs and start sharing that information freely but be mindful to put file and folder naming and organization protocols in place to prevent your central information space from becoming chaotic.

Tackle Time Zones

When you have staff on opposite ends of the earth, keeping regular team-wide work hours probably isn't realistic. However, if you have employees working with only a small time difference, try to agree on set hours for your team to work at the same time to avoid communication delays. No matter the time difference, always make deadlines according to one specific time zone, for instance, Eastern Standard Time.

Keep an Open Line of Regular Feedback and Updates

An open line of feedback and updates is crucial for virtual accountability. Managers and staff must be able to provide feedback freely and openly, just like they would in a physical office. Even if you are using virtual project management tools that offer transparency, schedule regular group, and individual feedback and progress update sessions. Regular check-ins generate communication and drive accountability.

Trust Your Employees

Just as you shouldn't hover over your employees to micromanage their work in a physical office, don't play prison warden online. I've already explained trust has a large part to play in accountability. Avoid the temptation to use remote monitoring apps and software that allows you to spy on your employees to make sure they're working. They aren't children who need policing to make sure they behave. You have to trust your team; just like they must trust you.

Judge Performance by Results

Remember that introverted employee who is probably reveling in the opportunity to avoid socializing by working remotely? You are going to have employees like that. You are also going to have parents who need to look after children and can't spend much time on virtual water cooler chats. Just because an employee doesn't have a strong virtual presence doesn't mean they're not diligently working away. Judge performance by results and not how active they are on various virtual platforms. How busy an employee appears to be doesn't translate into results. Let their actual work speak for itself.

Measure Accountability Realistically

You need to rethink how you judge accountability when your workspace goes virtual. What if the virtual platform crashes and communication becomes harder for a day or two? What if a deadline is missed because an employee suddenly has unstable internet connection because of inclement weather or maintenance in the area? These are things your staff cannot be held accountable for because they are out of their control. You need to develop realistic measures for accountability that are specific to working remotely. One thing you can hold your team accountable for because it is within their control is to communicate the difficulties they are experiencing so you're aware of the complications.

Virtual Team Building to Build Trust

Virtual team building to maintain workplace relationships and trust is even more important than when you work in a physical office. The isolation and sense of being disconnected from each other can take its toll and you need to find ways to bring your team together.

Share and Share Alike

This activity can be done while everybody is online at the same time if they are in similar time zones or separately if the time differences are large. It's pretty simple, pick something everybody needs to share. It could be:

- A picture of their home workspace.

- Introducing their pets, children, or partner.

- A video tour of their home or garden.

- A song they dig at the moment.

- A feel-good picture of anything they think will make others feel good.

The potential for this activity is almost endless. However, make sure everybody agrees on what they're sharing. Someone may not feel comfortable sharing a video tour of their home, for instance. Don't put this down to a majority vote, if any member of the team is uncomfortable with the suggestion of what to share, don't force them to do it; pick something everybody can agree on.

Trivia

This activity requires your team to be online at the same time and on a video conferencing call. Each person can look up trivia questions to ask the team and everybody takes turns asking their questions. You can decide whether you want the answering members of the team to collaborate to decide on the answer or if you want to bring in a competitive edge by awarding points to the first person to offer the correct answer to the question.

Deserted Island

You can play this game while everyone is online at the same time or separately across large time zone differences. The scenario is being stranded on a deserted island and you can only pick three items from a list to have with you. Get creative with the list; don't stick to only survival tools. Make sure your list is a decent length, too. The more items there are to choose from, the more fun the answers will be. Now comes the really fun part, you have to explain why you would have each of the items with you.

Conclusion

See, accountability is achievable, and confronting it doesn't have to be a veritable nightmare. Accountability is crucial to your personal and professional success. Building an accountable team is vital for organizational success. It is an undeniably essential trait and now you know how to achieve it.

I've provided you with all the knowledge and tools you need to start improving your personal accountability and the accountability of your staff today. I've given you questions to ask, assessments to perform, tips, advice, and activities to help you bring your team together and start holding themselves and each other accountable.

You also now know how to prepare for and carry out that difficult conversation about accountability when you're faced with someone who just won't take ownership of their actions. I've provided you with ways and means of improving emotional intelligence and assertiveness to help you tackle those accountability problems with others. You are now equipped to be more accountable and hold others accountable and there's nothing standing in your way. Have you already started using the knowledge you've gained to improve accountability? If not, what are you waiting for? Start making those changes today for a more accountable tomorrow.

References

(EI) Emotional intelligence questionnaire. (n.d.). Health Research Board. https://www.drugsandalcohol.ie/26776/1/Emotional_intelligence_questionnaire-LAL1.pdf

5 reasons why we make excuses. (n.d.) The Coaching Academy. https://www.the-coaching-academy.com/blog/2016/04/771

8 ways to keep your team accountable in a virtual environment. (2021, January 29). The Alternative Board. https://www.thealternativeboard.com/blog/8-ways-to-keep-your-employees-accountable-in-a-virtual-environment

Accountability - Overview, Key Roles, and Examples. (n.d.). Corporate Finance Institute. https://corporatefinanceinstitute.com/resources/careers/soft-skills/accountability/

Accountability is the key to building trust. (n.d.) Culture Partners. https://culture.io/accountability-is-the-key-to-building-trust/

Ackerman, C. (2020, January 9). *69 exercises for leading with emotional intelligence.* Positive Psychology.

https://positivepsychology.com/emotional-intelligence-leadership-effectiveness/

Ackerman, C. (2021, March 26). *13 emotional intelligence activities and exercises.* Positive Psychology. https://positivepsychology.com/emotional-intelligence-exercises/

Aguirre, C. (n.d.) *Why do we make excuses?* Headspace. https://www.headspace.com/articles/why-do-we-make-excuses

Aldana, S. (2021, April 8). *10 tips to implement mindfulness in the workplace.* Well Steps. https://www.wellsteps.com/blog/2020/02/11/mindfulness-in-the-workplace/

Amaresan, S. (2021, May 10). *27 conflict resolution skills to use with your team and your customers.* Hub Spot. https://blog.hubspot.com/service/conflict-resolution-skills

Amin, H. (2019, December 3). *How to make accountability a core part of your workplace culture.* Hyper Context. https://hypercontext.com/blog/management-skills/create-culture-accountability-workplace

Bell, A. (2020, June 23). *57 fun virtual team building activities, games, $ ideas to boost remote employee morale in online teams for 2021.* Snacknation. https://snacknation.com/blog/virtual-team-building/

Boesen, L. (2014). *Personal accountability self-assessment final.* www.lisaboesen.com/new/wp-content/uploads/2014/05/personal-accountability-self-assessment-final1.pdf

Bookspan, N. (n.d.). *Blameless problem solving and self-accountability.* Jaburg Wilk. http://www.jaburgwilk.com/news-publications/blameless-problem-solving-and-self-accountability

Calvert, D. (2016). *Leadership & Commitment: Are You Responsible or Accountable?* People First Productivity Solutions. https://blog.peoplefirstps.com/connect2lead/responsible-accountable

Cannarella, D. (2016). *Emotional intelligence coaching: Balance assertiveness, boost EI.* High performing Systems, Inc. https://www.hpsys.com/PDFs/EIatWorkSeriesBalancingAssertiveness.pdf

Caprino, K. (2013, November 4). *5 critical steps to fearless confrontation.* Forbes. https://www.forbes.com/sites/kathycaprino/2013/11/04/5-critical-steps-to-fearless-confrontation/?sh=98ebd312b4de

Caprino, K. (2013, November 4). *5 critical steps to fearless confrontation.* Forbes. https://www.forbes.com/sites/kathycaprino/201

3/11/04/5-critical-steps-to-fearless-
confrontation/?sh=98ebd312b4de

Chadwick, S. (2019, July 22). *Self-accountability: Essential but not enough?* Accountable 2 You. https://accountable2you.com/blog/self-accountability/

Craig, H. (2020, October 31). *10 ways to build trust in a relationship.* Positive Psychology. https://positivepsychology.com/build-trust/

Davidson, P. (2016, February 19). *5 ways to maintain accountability in your virtual workplace.* Ring Central. https://www.ringcentral.com/us/en/blog/5-ways-to-maintain-accountability-in-your-virtual-workplace/

Dinardi, G. (2020, May 21). *Virtual team communication: What is it, top challenges, & best practices.* Nextiva. https://www.nextiva.com/blog/virtual-team-communication.html

Employee accountability and performance metrics. (2018, October 26). Knowledge City Learning Solutions. https://www.knowledgecity.com/blog/employee-accountability/

Fielding, L. (2015, July 21). *Mindful assertiveness*: 3 simple steps. Huffpost. https://www.huffpost.com/entry/3-simple-steps-to-mindful_b_7828976

Finkelstein, D. (2020, November 23). *Why is being accountable so important?* Tick Those Boxes. https://tickthoseboxes.com.au/why-is-being-accountable-so-important/

Fouts, M. (2018, July 19). *Being mindful in your relationships.* Forbes. https://www.forbes.com/sites/forbescoachescouncil/2018/07/19/being-mindful-in-your-relationships/?sh=7e727bfcceaa

Franchetti, S. (2016, October 11). *Emotional intelligence and its impact on communication in the workplace.* Franchetti Communications. https://franchetti.com/emotional-intelligence-impact-communication-workplace/

Freedman, J. (2019, January 16). Creating a culture of accountability" The 4 checkpoints of accountable communication. Six Seconds. https://www.6seconds.org/2019/01/15/accountable-communication/

Frieden, K. (2016, November 9). *Just do it: How to identify and address 8 levels of accountability.* Kent State University. https://www.kent.edu/yourtrainingpartner/just-do-it-how-identify-and-address-8-levels-accountability

Gelles, D. (2019). *How to be more mindful at work.* The New York Times.

https://www.nytimes.com/guides/well/be-more-mindful-at-work

Goal setting and personal mission statement. (n.d.). The University of Akron. https://www.uakron.edu/armyrotc/MS1/13.pdf

Hansen, R. (n.d.). *The five-step plan for creating personal mission statements.* Live Career. https://www.livecareer.com/resources/careers/planning/creating-personal-mission-statements

Hauser, E. (2021, September 7). Why you remember things better when you write them down. Life Savvy. https://www.lifesavvy.com/19204/why-you-remember-things-better-when-you-write-them-down/

Heathfield, S. (2021, February 28). *10 tips for dealing with difficult people at work.* The Balance Careers. https://www.thebalancecareers.com/overcome-your-fear-of-confrontation-and-conflict-1917869

Heathfield, S. (2021, February 28). 1*0 tips for dealing with difficult people at work.* The Balance Careers. https://www.thebalancecareers.com/overcome-your-fear-of-confrontation-and-conflict-1917869

How accountability leads to successful management. (2021, March 10). Torch. https://torch.io/blog/how-accountability-leads-to-success/

How to maintain effective communication in a virtual workplace. (2020, November 4). Accounts One. https://accountantsone.com/effective-communication-in-virtual-workplace/

Insperity Staff. (2016, February 16). *How to inspire employees to give their best performance.* Insperity. https://www.insperity.com/blog/leadership-how-to-inspire-employees-to-give-their-best-performance-ever/

Insperity Staff. (2019, July). *How to improve accountability in the workplace in 5 steps.* Insperity. https://www.insperity.com/blog/improve-accountability-workplace-5-steps/

Izquierdo, R. (2021, January 17). *Top 5 employee performance metrics to track.* The Blueprint. https://www.fool.com/the-blueprint/performance-metrics/

Jack, L. (2020, November 12). *12 tips for handling difficult conversations at work.* ICS Learn. https://www.icslearn.co.uk/blog/posts/2020/november/12-tips-for-handling-difficult-conversations-at-work/

Kaboli-Nejad, S. (n.d.). *Seven questions to measure workplace accountability.* Culture Amp. https://www.cultureamp.com/blog/seven-questions-to-measure-workplace-accountability

Kappel, M. (2017, November 3). *6 strategies to resolve conflict at work.* Entrepreneur. https://www.entrepreneur.com/article/303617

Kruse, K. (n.d.) *Improve personal accountability: 12 things to do in 12 weeks.* Forbes. https://www.forbes.com/sites/kevinkruse/2020/01/13/improve-personal-accountability-12-things-to-do-in-12-weeks/?sh=3bfe40226e63

Kulhan, B. (2013, February 13). *Why "yes, and…" might be the most valuable phrase in business.* Big Think. https://bigthink.com/experts-corner/why-yes-and-might-be-the-most-valuable-phrase-in-business

Landry, L. (2019, April 3). *Why emotional intelligence is important in leadership.* Harvard Business School. https://online.hbs.edu/blog/post/emotional-intelligence-in-leadership

Lares, A. (2021, January 14). *Ten steps to conflict resolution success.* Shapiro Negotiations. https://www.shapironegotiations.com/ten-steps-to-conflict-resolution-success/

Lever Team. (2019, April 10). *Creating a culture of accountability.* Lever. https://www.lever.co/blog/creating-a-culture-of-accountability/

Management Training and Leadership Training — Online. (n.d.). Mind Tools.

https://www.mindtools.com/?pages/article/new LDR

Marchant, J. (2013, March 5). *Assertiveness.* Emotional Intelligence At Work. https://www.emotionalintelligenceatwork.com/resources/assertiveness/

Marom, S. (2018, May 7). *Accountability vs responsibility in project management.* Adobe Workfront. https://www.workfront.com/why-workfront

McCarthy, D. (2019, June 25). *How to build a culture of accountability.* The Balance Careers. https://www.thebalancecareers.com/how-to-build-a-culture-of-accountability-2275828

McCullough, C. (2019, December 6). *Growing team accountability in your organization.* Rhythm Systems. https://www.rhythmsystems.com/blog/growing-accountability-in-your-organization

McCullough, C. (2020, February 28). *Accountability tips: Quick tips for building accountability.* Rhythm Systems. https://www.rhythmsystems.com/blog/quick-tips-for-building-accountability

McCullough, C. (2020, January 6). *5 steps to having an accountability conversation (video).* Rhythm Systems. https://www.rhythmsystems.com/blog/5-steps-to-having-an-accountability-conversation

McCullough, C. (2020, July 30). *Building accountability into your culture: Does your team have an accountability problem?* Rhythm Systems. https://www.rhythmsystems.com/blog/assessment-do-you-have-a-team-accountability-problem

McCullough, C. (2020, June 25). *How does effective communication affect collaboration in organizational accountability?* Rhythm Systems. https://www.rhythmsystems.com/blog/the-link-between-communication-accountability

Merriam-Webster. (2019). *Definition of accountability.* Merriam-Webster.com. https://www.merriam-webster.com/dictionary/accountability

Miech, C. (2020, November 24). *Stay on track with these 10 employee performance metrics.* Track Time 24. https://tracktime24.com/Blog/employee-performance-metrics

Mihalicz, D. (2019, July 8). *What is accountability?* Effective Managers. https://effectivemanagers.com/dwight-mihalicz/what-is-accountability-part-1-of-the-effective-managerstm-understanding-accountability-series/

Nelson, E. (2020, June 25). *3 ways to promote accountability in the workplace.* Fond. https://www.fond.co/blog/accountability-in-the-workplace/

Nortje, A. (2021, August 2). *How to practice mindfulness: 11 practical steps and tips.* Positive Psychology. https://positivepsychology.com/how-to-practice-mindfulness/

Novakovic, A. (2019, February 14). *Difficult conversations with employees: 9 crucial rules to remember.* Insperity. https://www.insperity.com/blog/difficult-conversations-with-employees/

Oleniczak Brown, J. (2017, April 6). *Leading with a 'yes, and'.* Forbes. https://www.forbes.com/sites/forbescoachescouncil/2017/04/06/leading-with-a-yes-and/?sh=5328fc16588e

Olszewski, M. (2018, June 15). *Resolving conflict when others disappoint, step 1 – Is this worth discussing?* Atomic Object. https://spin.atomicobject.com/2018/06/15/conflict-resolution-when/

Page, O. (2021, August 17). *Transformational leadership: How to motivate & inspire teams.* Positive Psychology. https://positivepsychology.com/transformational-leadership/

Perez, D. (2021, August 22). *10 tips to make personal accountability come naturally.* Wild Simple Joy. https://wildsimplejoy.com/personal-accountability/

Prevention is better than cure. (n.d.) Oxford Reference. https://www.oxfordreference.com/view/10.1093/oi/authority.20110803100344375

Resolving conflict situations. (2019). Berkeley University of California. https://hr.berkeley.edu/hr-network/central-guide-managing-hr/managing-hr/interaction/conflict/resolving

Responsibility vs accountability – What's the difference? (2020, February 13). Sprigg HR. https://sprigghr.com/blog/hr-professionals/responsibility-vs-accountability-whats-the-difference/

Samuel, M. (2021, August 24). *8 behaviors that help develop personal accountability.* B State. https://bstate.com/2021/03/03/behaviors-that-help-develop-personal-accountability/

Schenck, L. (2011, December 5). *How to practice assertive listening.* Mindful Muse. https://www.mindfulnessmuse.com/interpersonal-relationships/how-to-practice-assertive-listening

Schenck, L. (2013, September 11). *Basic assertiveness skills for interpersonal effectiveness.* Mindful Muse. https://www.mindfulnessmuse.com/dialectical-behavior-therapy/basic-assertiveness-skills-for-interpersonal-effectiveness

Schmitz, T. (2016, June 3). *The importance of emotional awareness in communication.* Conover.

https://www.conovercompany.com/the-importance-of-emotional-awareness-in-communication/

Selva, J. (2021, July 23). *The quick guide to assertiveness: Become direct, firm, and positive.* Positive Psychology. https://positivepsychology.com/assertiveness/

Shite, A. (April 28). *10 authentic self evaluation phrases for accountability.* Via Maven. https://www.viamaven.com/blog/10-self-evaluation-phrases-accountability

Sicinski, A. (2018, December 10). Are you living a life of endless excuses? Here's how to stop! IQ Matrix. https://blog.iqmatrix.com/a-life-of-excuses

SMART goal – Definition, guide, and importance of goal setting. (2015). Corporate Finance Institute. https://corporatefinanceinstitute.com/resources/knowledge/other/smart-goal/

Sutton, J. (2020, December 16). *The importance of mindfulness: 20+ reasons to practice mindfulness.* Positive Psychology. https://positivepsychology.com/importance-of-mindfulness/

Sutton, J. (2021, August 12). *How to boost self-esteem: 12 simple exercises & CBT tools.* Positive Psychology. https://positivepsychology.com/self-esteem-boost-exercises/

Sutton, J. (2021, August 16). *How to perform assertiveness skills training: 6 exercises.* Positive Psychology. https://positivepsychology.com/assertiveness-training/

Sutton, J. (2021, August 18). *Assertiveness in leadership: 19 techniques for workplace managers.* Positive Psychology. https://positivepsychology.com/assertiveness-in-leadership/

Thakrar, M. (n.d.) *How to develop emotional intelligence using mindfulness.* Forbes. https://www.forbes.com/sites/forbescoachescouncil/2019/06/11/how-to-develop-emotional-intelligence-using-mindfulness/?sh=683d3d0d3f3a

The 5 C's of leadership accountability. (n.d.) Team Strength Inc. https://www.teamstrength.com/the-5-cs-of-leadership-accountability/

Tracy, B. (2017, October 30). *Why emotional intelligence is indispensable for leaders.* Forbes. https://www.forbes.com/sites/forbescoachescouncil/2017/10/30/why-emotional-intelligence-is-indispensable-for-leaders/

Trust vs accountability: What's the difference? (2020, May). Simply PHP. https://simplyphp.com/articles/trust-vs-accountability-whats-the-difference

Wai, F. (n.d.). *18 practical ways to build trust in the workplace.* Jostle. https://blog.jostle.me/blog/ways-to-build-trust-at-work

Wakeman, C. (n.d.). *Personal accountability and the pursuit of workplace happiness.* Forbes. https://www.forbes.com/sites/cywakeman/2015/10/26/personal-accountability-and-the-pursuit-of-workplace-happiness/?sh=217e2c811ca2

Why do people fight? (2018, December 24). Seeken. https://seeken.org/why-do-people-fight/

Why is accountability important in the workplace? (2020, December 22). Power DMS. https://www.powerdms.com/policy-learning-center/why-is-accountability-important-in-the-workplace

Why is accountability so important? (n.d.). Culture Partners. https://culture.io/why-is-accountability-so-important/

Wishart, J. (2019, January 29). *10 signs of an accountable culture (Infographic).* Rhythm Systems. https://www.rhythmsystems.com/blog/10-signs-of-an-accountable-culture-infographic

Zofi, Y. (2020, April 7). *10 rules for building trust and developing accountability on your virtual team.* Leadership Essentials. https://hcleadershipessentials.com/blogs/team-development/10-rules-for-building-trust-and-developing-accountability-on-your-virtual-team

zz8btPQw16. (2018, January 22). *Developing emotional intelligence – Part 5 – Assertiveness. The Learning Cog.* https://www.learningcog.com/developing-emotional-intelligence-part-5-assertiveness/

Made in United States
North Haven, CT
05 September 2024

57033216R00104